PSYCHOLOGY
IN MINUTES

MARCUS WEEKS

D0972918

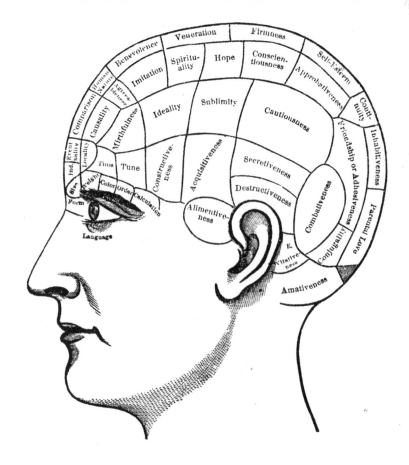

PSYCHOLOGY IN MINUTES

MARCUS WEEKS

Quercus

CONTENTS

Introduction   6
Foundations of psychology   8
Biological psychology   24
Behaviorism   46
Cognitive psychology   90
Psychoanalysis   142
Social psychology   186

Developmental psychology 236
Psychology of difference 286
Clinical psychology 342
Applications of psychology 384
Glossary 408
Index 412
Acknowledgments 416

Introduction

The story of psychology begins in Classical Greece. Plato and Aristotle argued over the existence of immortal souls, as well as the human capacity to experience, perceive, and think about things. Indeed, the word "psychology" itself derives from the ancient Greek *psyche*, meaning both "soul" and "mind." The study of the psyche remained a philosophical pursuit until comparatively recently. The first references to psychology as a distinct subject appear in the 17th century—Culpeper's *Complete Herbal* defined the discipline as the "knowledge of the soul." However, Curzon's 1712 description got closer to our modern conception of the subject, "Psychology examines the constitution of the Mind of Man, its Faculties, and Passions."

Today, psychology is considered to be the scientific study of mind and behavior. Its roots may be in philosophy, but it encompasses elements of physiology, medicine, and the social sciences. Psychology emerged as a science in its own right toward the end of the 19th century, alongside the emerging fields of neuroscience and sociology—with which it has more than a passing connection.

The human mind, and human behavior, are complex and unpredictable. Different approaches to the study of psychology emerged in the 20th century, and it became obvious that the "study of mind and behavior" covered a vast and varied field. Some psychologists approached the subject as they would a natural science, observing and experimenting in laboratories. Others saw it more as a clinical science, which could produce benefits for those with disorders of the mind or problems in behavior. Different branches also emerged, studying the behavior of people in social groups, the ways in which our minds develop as we grow up, and even the things that make us unique individuals.

Psychology today covers all these areas and more—it examines the ways our minds work and how we act and react in the world around us. Like any science, as well as giving us an insight into the workings of our minds, psychology has provided a multitude of applications, from clinical therapy through to social policy, management, and advertising. It is a vast subject and one that never fails to fascinate.

Precursors of psychology

The natural sciences (astronomy, physics, chemistry, biology, and earth sciences) evolved from philosophical speculation about the nature of the world, but it wasn't until the 19th century that a scientific study of the way we think and behave emerged. One of the reasons for this was that, since we cannot have direct access to what is going on in other people's minds, a philosophy of the mind tended to be a matter of introspection and lacked the objectivity of a true science.

Furthermore, the strictly physical study of the brain—although objectively scientific—told us little about how we think and behave. Some physiologists, in Germany in particular, turned their attention to the study of mental processes, and at much the same time philosophers (especially in the USA), adopted a more rigorously scientific approach to the philosophy of the mind. From these two different approaches, the new science of psychology emerged as a distinct scientific discipline, bridging the gap between philosophy and physiology.

Mind and brain

In many cultures around the world, there is the belief that humans have a soul (often immortal) that exists independently of the body. For Greek philosophers, the soul, or psyche, was also seen as the seat of our ability to reason— what we would call the mind today. While Aristotle and his followers saw body and soul as inseparable, Plato believed that the psyche belonged in the eternal world of ideas, separate from the material world our bodies inhabit.

Later philosophers, notably the Islamic scholar Avicenna and the great mathematician and philosopher René Descartes, proposed that the immaterial mind and material body are separate entities. This mind–body dualism was challenged by Gilbert Ryle in 1949, who dismissed the idea of an independently existing soul or mind as seeing a "ghost in the machine." More recently, computer technology has presented a useful analogy: brain and mind can be seen in terms of hardware and software, which are distinct but interdependent.

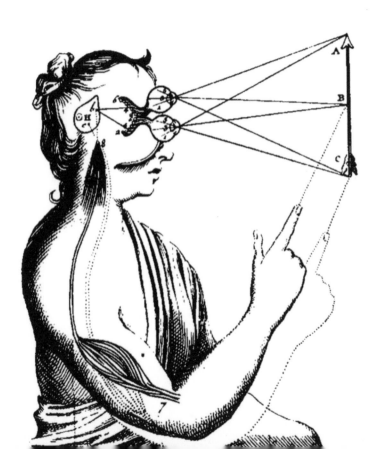

Neuroscience

Around the middle of the 19th century, medical science was turning its attention to disorders of the central nervous system. Early neurologists, including Jean-Martin Charcot, examined and described conditions, such as multiple sclerosis, prompting research into the physiology of the nervous system. A turning point came with the staining technique devised by Camillo Golgi, which made it possible to examine individual cells under a microscope.

Santiago Ramón y Cajal, the founder of modern neuroscience, used this technique to identify and categorize the nerve cells of the nervous system and brain (now called neurons). Later research showed that neurons "communicate" with one another via electrochemical signals, passing information from the sensory organs to the brain. It also became clear that electrochemical activity between neurons within the brain is associated with mental processes, leading to a distinctly physiological approach to psychology.

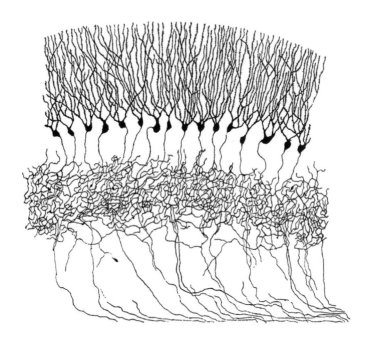

Some of the earliest images of nerve cells in the brain were drawn by
Spanish neurologist Santiago Ramón y Cajal.

Hypnosis

German doctor Franz Mesmer rose to fame in the late 18th century for his therapy using magnets to restore the balance of a patient's "animal magnetism." During the treatment—later known as mesmerism—some of his patients went into a trancelike state, which they claimed relieved their symptoms. A contemporary of Mesmer, a Portuguese-Goan monk called Abbé Faria, realized that the key was not the magnets, but the "lucid sleep" that made the patient more susceptible to the power of suggestion. His technique of inducing a mental state of heightened suggestibility, later dubbed "hypnosis" by the surgeon James Braid, aroused considerable interest in the 19th century, both as a therapy and a form of entertainment. The pioneering neurologist Jean-Martin Charcot adopted hypnotism as part of his treatment of hysteria, a practice continued by his students Josef Breuer and Sigmund Freud. From their use of hypnotism, Freud went onto develop a "talking cure" and his theories of the unconscious and psychoanalysis (see pages 144, 146, and 142).

Medical conditions

Throughout history, mental disorders have been treated with suspicion and even fear. Severe conditions were often attributed to some form of possession, while disorders such as "melancholy" were thought to be an imbalance of humors, and hysteria caused by problems of the uterus. For a long time, these conditions were considered incurable. Sufferers were branded "insane" and locked in institutions, such as the notorious Bedlam.

Neurologists, such as Charcot, believed that many mental disorders were in fact illnesses with a physical cause (see page 12). This idea was taken up by other physicians, including Emil Kraepelin, who in 1883 published his *Textbook of Psychiatry*. In it, he gave a detailed classification of mental illnesses, including "dementia praecox" (schizophrenia), which he attributed to physical abnormalities in the brain. Kraepelin laid the foundations for the modern field of psychiatry (see page 324), and the medical classification and treatment of mental disorders.

In Hieronymus Bosch's 1494 painting *Cutting the Stone*, the "stone of madness" is removed from a patient suffering a mental disorder. The painting hints that the doctor does not know whether the problem is physical, spiritual, or psychological.

Beginnings of experimental psychology

One of the most prominent figures in the establishment of psychology as a distinct scientific subject was the German physiologist Wilhelm Wundt. His interest in psychology began after graduating in medicine and working as an assistant to Hermann von Helmholtz at the University of Heidelberg, researching human sensory perception. Later, at Leipzig University, he gave lectures on psychology, published perhaps the first psychology textbook and, in 1879, set up the first ever experimental psychology laboratory.

His aim was to apply scientific methodology to the study of the mind, which for him meant the study of consciousness and perception. Under strict laboratory conditions, he observed and measured responses of his human subjects to various sensations, and noted their own reports of their experiences. His insistence on experiments that could be controlled and replicated exactly set the standard for experimental psychology, firmly establishing its scientific credentials.

Pavlov's dogs

One of the turning points in the history of psychology came about by chance. And it was made by a physiologist, not an experimental psychologist. In the 1890s, the Russian Ivan Pavlov, researching the physical workings of the gastric systems of dogs, devised a method of collecting and measuring their saliva to ascertain its role in digestion. He noticed that salivation was not simply a response to the physical presence of food; the dogs also salivated in anticipation of food, or at the thought of food—a psychological stimulus.

Changing the tack of his experiments to explore this phenomenon, he discovered the principle of conditioning, a cornerstone of behaviorism—the approach that was to dominate psychology for the next half-century (see page 46). Pavlov's experiments also demonstrated that something as seemingly complex as animal behavior could be studied by experiment in the laboratory under controlled conditions, rather than merely observed in the natural world.

A wide range

During the 20th century, the new science of psychology developed into a broad discipline, branching into social and developmental psychology, the psychology of individual differences, and clinical psychology. In the USA, a new generation of psychologists, inspired by Pavlov's experiments, rejected philosophical examination of mental processes in favor of a scientific study of behavior. Meanwhile, in Europe, Freud's theories of the unconscious and psychoanalysis were proving very influential, but were seen by many to be unscientific.

German psychologists in particular followed in the tradition of Wilhelm Wundt's experimental psychology, studying perception, and countering behaviorism and Freud's psychodynamic approach with a movement known as Gestalt psychology (see page 110). This emphasis on cognitive processes rather than behavior became dominant in the second half of the century, alongside a renewed interest in biopsychology (see page 24) influenced by advances in brain-imaging techniques.

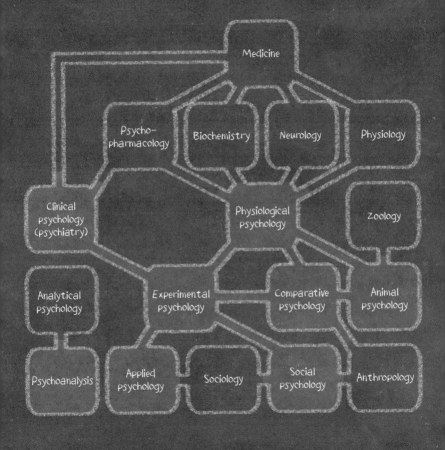

Biological psychology

Modern neuroscience—the study of the nervous system—
emerged as a branch of physiology at much the same time
as psychology was recognized as a distinct scientific subject.
The two disciplines have evolved side by side, and advances in
our knowledge of the physical workings of the nervous system,
and in particular the brain, have given rise to a branch of
psychology known as biopsychology, or biological psychology.

Also referred to as behavioral neuroscience, physiological
psychology, and psychobiology, this approach examines the
way in which the structure and functions of the brain affect
our mental processes and behavior—the connection between
the nervous system's "hardware" and "software." Advances
in neuroscience have given valuable insight into mental
processes, such as consciousness and perception, which have
only previously been studied introspectively. Modern brain-
imaging technology is enabling an even deeper understanding
of the role the brain's physiology plays in psychology.

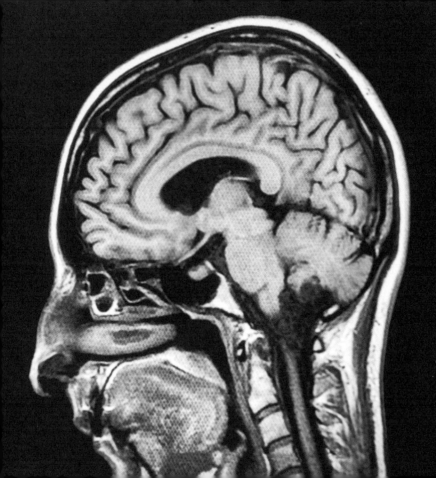

The brain and nervous system

Although the heart has been traditionally viewed as the "seat of the soul," the ancient Egyptians recognized that the brain is the home of the mind. Even for mind–body dualists, who believe the immaterial mind and physical body to be quite separate, the brain is where the two communicate (René Descartes believed that mind and body met in the pineal gland in the center of the brain). In biopsychological terms, however, a better explanation is that the brain and nervous system are the interface, not between our mental and physical selves, but between our selves and the external world.

Information from the sensory organs is transmitted to the brain, and "instructions" from the brain are sent back to control our actions and behavior. As well as enabling us to interact with the outside world, the brain's neural networks deal with incoming data, and are associated with our consciousness, experience, and perception, as well as thought processes, such as reasoning and decision-making.

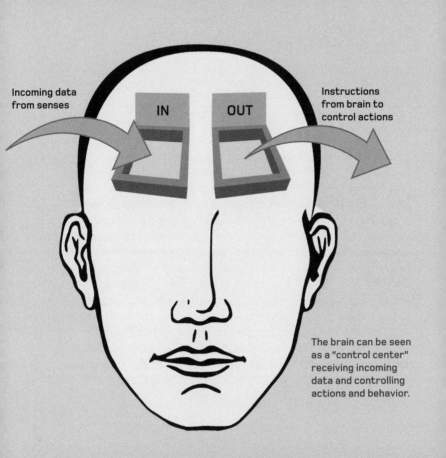

Incoming data from senses

Instructions from brain to control actions

IN

OUT

The brain can be seen as a "control center" receiving incoming data and controlling actions and behavior.

Neural pathways

Nerve cells, or neurons, are the building blocks of the nervous system. They pass information in the form of electrochemical impulses "fired" across the synapse—the gap at the junction between neurons. These electrochemical signals excite or inhibit the receiving neurons, "instructing" them whether or not to fire and pass on a message. This selective transmission of information sets up distinctive channels of communication, neural pathways, that together form a complex neural network. Some 80 percent of the 100 billion or so neurons in the human body are in the brain itself, allowing countless different neural pathways. The brain's various functions—sensory experiences, coordination, and movement, and "higher functions," such as perception, language, and reasoning—each show particular patterns of neural activity across different areas of the brain. Only recently have brain-imaging techniques allowed neuroscientists to examine this activity in detail and it has become obvious that we still have a lot to learn about its complexity.

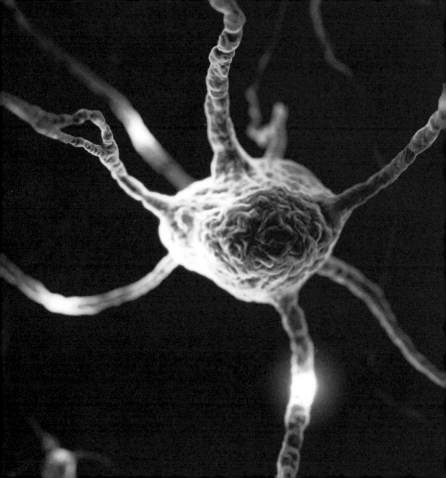

Sensory processes

We get our information about the external world from our sensory organs, especially our eyes, ears, noses, tongues, and skin. Specialized nerve cells, which have evolved to be excited by particular external stimuli, such as light or sound, provide the raw material of our sense experience. The stimulated receptor cells, also called afferent neurons, set up a chain reaction, exciting neighboring cells to create a neural pathway along "connector neurons" to the central nervous system and the brain. Signals from the brain travel on similar pathways to efferent neurons, also called motor or effector neurons, to stimulate muscles and control bodily movement.

Normally we are not aware of this process. However, when the brain is damaged, for example by a stroke, it can affect the use of perfectly healthy parts of our bodies—signals to them are not being sent. Conversely, amputees often experience "phantom limb phenomenon," when the brain is "tricked" into receiving signals from neural pathways that no longer exist.

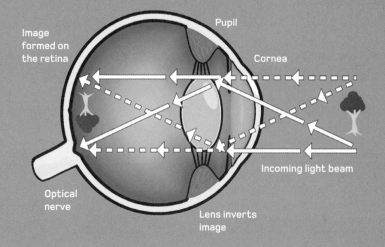

Specialized afferent neurons on the back wall
of the eye are sensitive to light.

Areas of the brain

In the brain, electrochemical "messages" from the sensory organs are experienced as sensation. Each of the senses sends a different kind of signal, and different areas of the brain—analogous to the different sensory organs—process them. At the rear of the brain, for example, information from our eyes is received by the primary visual cortex, and analyzed and interpreted by the neighboring visual association cortex.

Other areas, such as the auditory cortex and sensory cortex, work similarly, receiving and processing information. In addition, there are specialized areas associated with producing and understanding language (Broca's and Wernicke's areas—see page 34), and controlling voluntary movements (the primary motor cortex and premotor cortex). In the frontal lobe of our brains is the prefrontal cortex, which is associated with the higher mental functions—thinking and reasoning, personality and intelligence, planning, and decision-making.

Functional areas of the brain

1 Frontal lobe
Higher mental functions,
e.g. concentration,
planning and judgment
2 Motor function area
Eye movement and
orientation
3 Broca's area
Coordination of
speech muscles
4 Temporal lobe
Short-term memory
and emotion
5 Motor function area
Control of voluntary
muscles

6 Sensation area
Sensation from
muscles and skin
7 Somatosensory
association area
Touch sense and
object recognition
8 Wernicke's area
Language
comprehension
9 Auditory area
Hearing
10 Visual cortex
Vision

11 Cerebellum
Movement, balance, and
posture
12 Brainstem
Involuntary muscle
control, e.g. breathing
and blood pressure

Brain damage and what it can tell us

The first real evidence that functions are localized in the brain came from examination of patients with damage to specific parts of their brains. A famous case was Phineas P. Gage, an American railroad worker who in 1848 survived an accident that destroyed much of his left frontal lobe. Although he continued to lead a normal life, his personality changed dramatically. A few years later, physiologist Paul Broca conducted autopsies on patients with severe speech disorders, and discovered damage to a specific part of their brains (now known as Broca's area). Carl Wernicke similarly discovered the area associated with understanding language. More recently, while treating epilepsy sufferers, Roger Sperry recognized that the two halves of the brain have different functions. Each hemisphere processes sensory information from the opposite side of the body; the left hemisphere is linked to logical analysis, while the right deals in creative thinking. Research by Karl Lashley has shown that when a part of the brain is damaged, other parts can often take over.

Psychologist Oliver Sacks described the unusual neurological conditions suffered by his patients in his book *The Man Who Mistook His Wife for a Hat.*

Consciousness

Knowledge of the physiology of the nervous system tells us a great deal about how information from the senses is transmitted to and from the brain. However, comparatively little is known about how we experience those sensations, and what it is like to feel, think, and move. Consciousness is notoriously difficult to define, and explanations of it have tended to be in philosophical, introspective terms. William James (pictured), a philosopher as well as a pioneering psychologist, coined the phrase "stream of consciousness" in 1892 to describe the continuous process of thought and perception.

Each of us knows what it is to be conscious, but how do we recognize and measure this in others? They of course can tell us of their experience, but this is as subjective as our own experience. Medical criteria for consciousness are based on responses to sensory stimulus, but tell us nothing of a person's self-awareness. Examination of brain activity in various states of consciousness does, however, provide some clues.

What's happening in
the conscious brain?

Many of the advances in neuroscience were made possible by the invention of noninvasive means of examining activity within the brain, such as the electroencephalogram (EEG) and magnetic resonance imaging (MRI). It was soon discovered there are degrees of consciousness, ranging from fully awake, through daydreaming, trances, and sleeping, to being under anesthetic or in a vegetative state, and there is a great deal of electrical activity in each. Research into consciousness was pioneered by Francis Crick, who in 1995 noticed more activity in the prefrontal cortex of conscious brains when compared with unconscious brains, and concluded that this was the area associated with consciousness. Other biopsychologists, however, disagree with this "localization" of consciousness. Some mental functions, notably memory, are not confined to any single part of the brain. Consciousness, especially in the theory proposed by Giulio Tononi, comes from the interconnection of the various parts of our brains that deal with our senses, memories, and thoughts.

Waking and sleeping

We spend about a third of every day asleep, often in continuous eight-hour stretches—although many cultures have different habits, and there is evidence that at certain times in history, nightly sleep was routinely taken in two chunks. Whatever the pattern of sleep and wakefulness, however, it is usually regular. We appear to have an internal "body clock" that regulates this circadian rhythm.

In 1962, French cave explorer Michel Siffre spent two months underground with no contact with the surface, and discovered that he naturally fell into a 25-hour daily pattern. It is clear that we need to sleep on a regular basis and disturbing this daily rhythm is harmful physically and psychologically—jet lag, recurrent illness among shift workers, and the use of sleep deprivation as a means of torture amply demonstrate these effects. However, psychologists disagree about the purpose of sleep, whether it is physically or psychologically restorative, or serves some other evolutionary function.

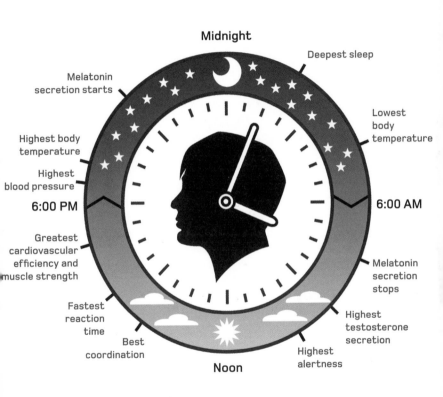

What happens when we are sleeping?

During sleep, our bodies are relatively inactive and we have limited awareness of the outside world, but our brains remain active and we pass through different degrees of consciousness in recurrent cycles. On falling asleep, we sink rapidly into successively deeper stages of sleep, but after about 90 minutes the process reverses, to a point where brain activity resembles the waking state. This stage is characterized by rapid eye movements (REM), but although the brain is very active, the muscles of the body are paralyzed and waking someone is harder than at any other stage. We typically go through three or four cycles of alternating REM and non-REM sleep each night, and each time the non-REM periods become shorter and less deep, while the periods of REM sleep lengthen. It is during REM sleep that we dream. Deprivation of REM sleep has been shown to cause "REM rebound"—longer and more frequent REM sleep later in the cycle—suggesting that one purpose of sleep is to dream, perhaps to sort out our thoughts and prepare our brains for new input.

SLEEP CYCLE

1 Interim between consciousness and sleep

REM sleep

Move to stage 2 after 5 to 15 minutes

2 Heart rate slows and brain does less complicated tasks

5 Increase in eye movement, heart rate, breathing, blood pressure, and temperature

After another 15 mins move into non-REM sleep Delta stage

Move into REM sleep approximately 90 mins after first feeling sleepy

4 Body temperature and blood pressure decrease

Deep restful sleep

3 Body makes repairs

Motivation: needs and drives

As well as physiological needs for survival—air to breathe, food and drink, warmth, shelter, and protection from predators—there are psychological drives that shape our behavior. The physiologist Walter Cannon explained this in terms of the body's need to find a stable balance, so that we are driven to eat, for example, by the physical needs of an empty stomach, an idea refined by psychologist Clark Hull in his 1943 "drive reduction theory"—that all our behavior is to satisfy the drives caused by our primary needs.

Other psychologists recognized that we have more than simply physiological needs. Our behavior is complex, and is shaped by multiple psychological drives to satisfy both social and cognitive needs. In 1943, Abraham Maslow identified a hierarchy of human needs, ranging from the basic physical needs of deficiency and survival, through those of security, and the need for friendship, family, and intimacy, to a need for esteem and achievement (see pages 170, 172, and 354).

Human motivations are complex and range from basic physiological necessities to "higher" psychological needs—for example, the social drives that compel people to commute day after day.

Behaviorism

The behaviorist approach arose from the desire to make psychology a truly scientific discipline. Psychologists at the beginning of the 20th century were anxious to move away from philosophical speculation about the mind and establish objective methods of studying our psychological makeup. Many US psychologists believed that the mind could be understood by observing its interaction with the world in behavior.

At the heart of the behaviorist approach was the idea that behavior is a response to a stimulus, a notion reinforced by physiologist Ivan Pavlov's experiments (see page 20). The experimental methods of physiology, especially using animals, provided a framework for behaviorist psychologists but, more importantly, Pavlov's work also provided a central theme for behaviorism—the principle of conditioning (see page 50). Behaviorist psychology developed not only as the study of human and animal behavior, but as a theory of how behavior is learned through stimulus and response by conditioning.

An objective approach

One of the major obstacles in getting psychology recognized as a branch of science was the abstract nature of the mind. In order to establish its scientific credentials, psychologists needed to adopt scientific methodology, including observation and experimentation. Because we only have direct access to our own minds, our observation of mental processes is introspective and necessarily subjective, but science demands an objective approach.

A solution adopted by behaviorist psychologists is not to attempt to examine the mind's workings, but to observe how they manifest themselves in behavior. Not only can behavior of animals and humans be observed, but the behavioral response of an animal to a specific situation can be examined under strict laboratory conditions—allowing experiments to be replicated. Thanks to this objective scientific approach, behaviorism, and its theories of stimulus and response, dominated experimental psychology until the mid-20th century.

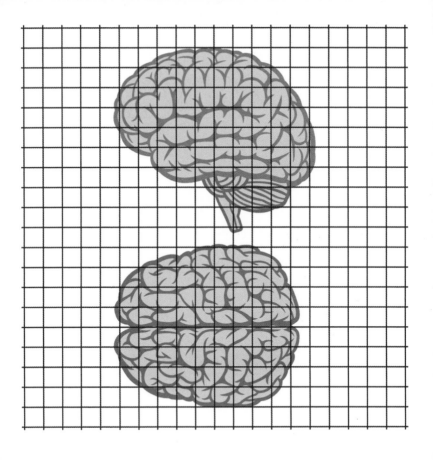

Classical conditioning

The impetus for the largely US behaviorist movement was neither American nor a psychologist. Ivan Pavlov was a Russian physiologist researching the salivating response of dogs to the stimulus of food. The dogs in his experiments salivated when presented with food, but he noticed that over time they learned to associate the approach of a lab assistant with food, and they salivated at his appearance. This, he reasoned, was a response to a psychological rather than physical stimulus. When he sounded a bell each time food was offered to the dogs, he found the dogs would salivate at the sound of the bell, even when no food appeared. This was as a result of what he called conditioning. Before conditioning, the food represented an unconditioned stimulus, which prompted the unconditioned response of salivation; the neutral signal of ringing a bell produced no response. During conditioning, the food and bell together prompted the same unconditioned response, but after conditioning, the bell alone—a conditioned stimulus—elicited the conditioned response of salivation.

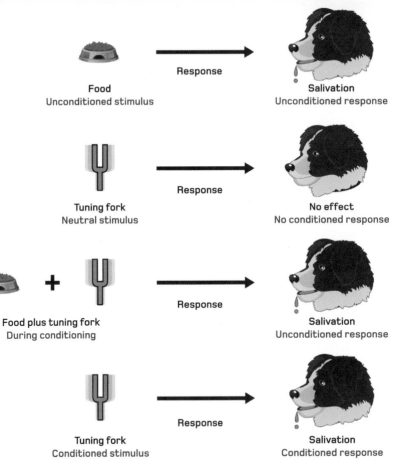

Puzzle boxes

American psychologist Edward Thorndike was a pioneer of experimental behaviorist psychology. He broke new ground by devising experiments using mazes and gadgets of his own design, known as "puzzle boxes," to study the behavior of laboratory animals. In this, he was following in Pavlov's footsteps, but his experiments led to a different interpretation of the principle of conditioning (see page 54).

In a typical experiment, a hungry cat was put into a puzzle box—a cage with a simple lever inside that released the catch of the door. A bowl of food was then put outside the box where the cat could see it, and the time taken for the cat to discover and work the lever was noted, and the experiment repeated at intervals and with different cats. Where Pavlov's work had involved training his dogs to associate a neutral signal with a stimulus, Thorndike's puzzle boxes were designed to allow his feline subjects to discover for themselves what behavior produced a reward.

Edward Thorndike's puzzle box

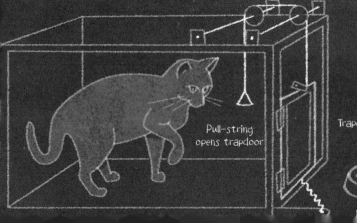

Pull-string
opens trapdoor

Trapdoor

Reward

Positive and negative conditioning

Thorndike's experiments provided the template for almost all subsequent behaviorist experiments. The model of presenting an experimental subject with a specific stimulus or task under controlled conditions became known as "instrumental conditioning"—as opposed to "classical" (Pavlovian) conditioning, where association between two stimuli is imposed to elicit a conditioned response.

In repeated and increasingly complex puzzle-box experiments, Thorndike discovered what was to become a basic principle of behaviorism. He observed that the cats initially found the means of escape by accident, while exploring their environment, but in repeat experiments took a shorter and shorter time to do so. He concluded that they gradually made the connection between action and outcome, repeating actions that produced a desired result (positive conditioning) and not repeating those that did not (negative conditioning). Unrewarded acts, as he put it, are stamped out—and rewarded responses "stamped in."

Animals operate levers to receive food, learning tasks from the outcomes of their actions.

The Law of Effect

In 1905, Thorndike formalized the findings of his experiments in the so-called Law of Effect. This is often stated as: behavior that produces a pleasant outcome in a particular situation is likely to be repeated in the same situation, and behavior that produces unpleasant consequences is less likely to be repeated. In fact, this is only half the story, as Thorndike emphasized the association between response and outcome, which is strengthened or weakened depending on whether the behavior is rewarded or profitless.

An association followed by a satisfying outcome will be strengthened but, if followed by a discomforting consequence, it will be weakened. Additionally, the more an association is used the stronger it becomes. Thorndike further theorized that the amount of satisfaction from rewarded actions would be equal in effect to the dissatisfaction of unrewarded ones, but in practice discovered that reward has more influence on behavior than either failure or even punishment.

Once bitten,
twice shy

Behaviorist Manifesto

In 1913 John B. Watson, chair of the psychology department at Johns Hopkins University, gave a lecture that became known as the "Behaviorist Manifesto." In it, he advocated abandoning "all talk of mental states," and proposed that the only truly scientific psychology was the study of behavior. His stance was radical but influential, and established psychology, in the USA at least, as the study of behavior rather than mind. Watson not only felt that it was impossible to study mental states objectively, he also believed that a "mental life" does not exist. For this reason, he rejected the Law of Effect (see page 56) with its emphasis on the learning process of association and based his behaviorism on classical Pavlovian conditioning— prompting a conditioned response from a conditioned stimulus.

Where Pavlov's experiments had been based on an involuntary physical response, Watson felt that emotional responses were more powerful influences on behavior. He believed that we have three fundamental emotions—fear, rage, and love—and that we can be conditioned to feel them in response to a stimulus.

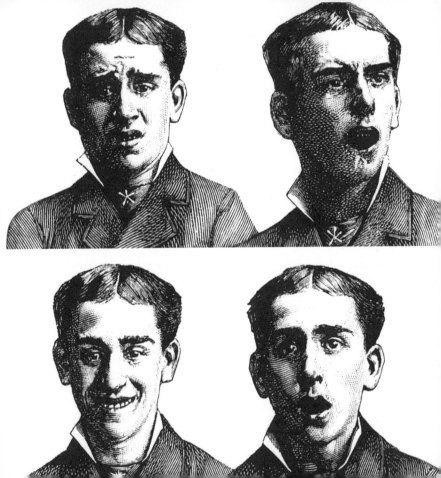

The Little Albert experiment

John B. Watson's most famous series of experiments was conducted in 1920 on a nine-month-old child, "Albert B." Watson set out to test his theory that classical conditioning could be used to teach an emotional response to a neutral stimulus. Albert, a healthy but reportedly rather unemotional child, was presented with various animals, including a dog, a rabbit, and a white rat, and with masks (with and without hair), and cotton wool. His reactions were generally of interest but not fear.

Later, Albert was presented with the rat again, but each time he reached out to touch it, Watson or his assistant made a loud noise, making the child cry in distress. After repeating this over a two-week period, Watson introduced the rat again, without the noise, and Albert started crying as soon as he saw it. And Watson discovered in further sessions that the child reacted similarly to all furry creatures, even a fur coat, or Watson wearing a mask with a cotton-wool beard.

A blank slate

At the time of Watson's advocacy of behaviorist psychology, many of his contemporaries were supporting the idea of eugenics. Watson, however, opposed the idea, coming down firmly on the side of nurture in the nature vs. nurture debate (see page 238). Human behavior, he believed, is shaped by conditioning, not inherited characteristics; we are all born a "blank slate."

He even boasted that given a dozen healthy infants and a level playing field, he could train any of them to become a specialist in any field—regardless of the individual's talents, abilities, or race. Although he admitted he was overstating his case, he believed the principle stood true—that stimulus-response conditioning is the way that we learn and it can be used to shape behavior. More controversially, in his famous "manifesto" lecture, Watson explicitly said that the goal of behaviorism is not the study but the "prediction and control of behavior."

Watson famously said, "Give me a dozen healthy infants, well-formed, and my own specified world to bring them up in and I'll guarantee to take any one at random and train him to become any type of specialist I might select."

A behaviorist's guide to bringing up baby

Shortly after the Little Albert experiment, Watson was forced to give up his academic post when it was discovered he was having an affair with his assistant, Rosalie Rayner. He took a job in advertising, where his application of psychology led to a very successful career. At the same time, he began writing books and articles on childcare, based on his interpretation of behaviorism. Watson believed that no behavior is innate and inherited, but learned through a process of stimulus and response as we interact with the world, and child development a matter of behavior being shaped by conditioning. Bringing up children is therefore a question of controlling the stimulus-response associations they make, which parents do by supervising their environment. Watson, who believed in the power of fundamental emotions of fear, rage, and love, advocated an objective, scientific approach to parenting, and even emotional detachment. This idea was enthusiastically taken up by a generation of young parents, but was later shown to do more psychological harm than good.

John B. Watson's attempts to create a scientific method of parenting set up a somewhat stiff relationship between parent and child, with overtones of strict Victorian attitudes.

Experimental ethics

Although Watson is often considered the founding father of behaviorism, his contribution to psychology is controversial. Moving from experiments on animals to humans —and the Little Albert experiment in particular—raises many ethical questions. Little was done to safeguard Albert B., nor was any attempt made to "uncondition" him or monitor his psychological health following the experiment.

Quite apart from that, he was only nine months old, so could not give his consent—and neither could the children whose parents followed Watson's misguided childcare advice. But because of the attention the experiments attracted, experimental psychologists were forced to consider their responsibilities and design more ethical experiments. Behaviorists reverted to animal subjects (although the ethics of animal experimentation were later also questioned). Where it was felt necessary to use people, the rule of thumb became that the subjects should be willing adults.

Cognitive behaviorism

In contrast to Watson's strict interpretation of behavior as a result of stimulus-response conditioning, Edward Tolman recognized that learning involves some thought processes, too. Tolman was a committed behaviorist but he had spent some time studying Gestalt psychology (see page 110) in Germany, and had become interested in cognition and mental processes.

Using rats in mazes, Tolman showed that learned behavior is not simply an automatic response. Rats in one group were given a reward for successfully negotiating the maze, while other groups were allowed to explore the maze without reward. When the second group were offered a reward, they found their way around the maze more quickly and with fewer mistakes than the others. He concluded that they had made a "mental map" of the maze without the stimulus of reward. Tolman believed that we humans, too, build a cognitive map of our environment, which we can later call upon—a process he called latent learning, in contrast to trial-and-error behavior.

Unlike many psychologists of the day, Edward Tolman believed the approaches of behaviorism and Gestalt psychology were not mutually exclusive.

A single lesson

Classical conditioning was based on Pavlov's discovery that a repeated combination of a stimulus and a neutral signal would eventually produce a conditioned response. Although subsequent behaviorist psychologists refined and extended the idea, it was widely accepted that repetition was necessary to reinforce the association. But not all behaviorists agreed. Edwin Guthrie, a firm believer in the behaviorism proposed by Thorndike, nevertheless felt that the association between an action and its outcome was established the first time it was made. He pointed out that after only one visit, a rat will return to a source of food it has found. In puzzle-box experiments, he noticed that cats made an immediate association between activating a mechanism and escape—a "one-trial learning" that they repeat. Guthrie explained this as learning "a movement": a combination of related movements becomes an act and, together, acts constitute behavior. Repetition is not necessary to reinforce the association of movement with outcome, but leads to the formation of acts that we recognize as behavior.

Radical behaviorism

B.F. Skinner's talent for self-publicity, coupled with his image as an eccentric inventor of gadgets, helped to make him perhaps the best known of behaviorist psychologists. His contribution to psychology was far from trivial, however, and he took a rigorously scientific approach to his work. In the spirit of Pavlov and Watson, he proposed a "radical behaviorism" to test behaviorist theories under strict conditions—dismissing anything that could not be observed, measured, and replicated in experiment.

In Skinner's radical approach, mental processes have no place in science as they cannot be observed objectively. He wanted to counter the idea hinted at by Thorndike's and Tolman's theories that thought processes play a part in stimulus-response conditioning. Radical behaviorism proposes that our behavior is conditioned solely by responses to our environment. Skinner believed that free will is an illusion and that all our actions and behavior are controlled by the selection of outcomes.

Operant conditioning

The most influential idea to come from Skinner's radical behaviorist approach was his theory of operant conditioning—that behavior is conditioned by the consequences of actions. Despite his admiration for Pavlov and Watson, he felt that behavior is not typically learned through the association of an action with a coincident or preceding stimulus, and that this classical conditioning was something of a special and rather artificial case.

His experiments, following in Thorndike's tradition, used animals in specially designed devices, which allowed them to explore their environment and discover the actions that produced a reward. Skinner concluded that the consequences of an action are what is crucial to learning behavior—an organism operates on its environment (hence "operant conditioning"), and encounters a stimulus that reinforces that operant behavior. The crucial difference between this and classical conditioning is that it involves the subject's active participation.

	Something is given to dog	Something is taken from dog
Increases likelihood of behavior being repeated	POSITIVE REINFORCEMENT (+R)	NEGATIVE REINFORCEMENT (−R)
Decreases likelihood of behavior being repeated	POSITIVE DISCOURAGEMENT (+P)	NEGATIVE DISCOURAGEMENT (+P)

Positive and negative reinforcement

Operant conditioning explains how we learn behavior through our interaction with our environment. The major factor in learning behavior, according to Skinner, is the reinforcement given by the consequence of an action. Positive outcomes, such as the delivery of food, or escape from a box, encourage the repetition of the action that brought it about, reinforcing the likelihood of that behavior in the future. Actions resulting in negative outcomes, such as pain or remaining confined, discourage repetition of the action.

Skinner was careful not to use the words "reward" and "punishment" to describe consequences, as he felt they had connotations of good and bad behavior—desirable or undesirable actions. Positive reinforcement can just as easily encourage "bad behavior"—for example, a thief who continues to get away with his crimes. Equally, "good behavior" can be discouraged by negative reinforcement, such as lending money to a needy friend who never pays you back.

Skinner boxes

Skinner arrived at his theory of operant conditioning from a number of different experiments involving animals in various devices of his own invention. These gadgets, which became known as Skinner boxes, were similar to Thorndike's puzzle boxes (see page 52), but were often more sophisticated.

Each Skinner box was an enclosed space containing a bar, button, or lever that could be operated by the experimental subject. The animal is free to explore the inside of the box and to discover the consequence of operating the mechanism. In a simple case, pressing on a bar might release a food pellet or give the animal a mild electric shock. In other boxes, the floor was electrified and the subject had to operate a switch to prevent receiving a shock. Skinner concluded that positive reinforcement has a stronger effect than negative reinforcement and increases the likelihood of an action being repeated. Prevention of a negative outcome also acts as a form of positive reinforcement.

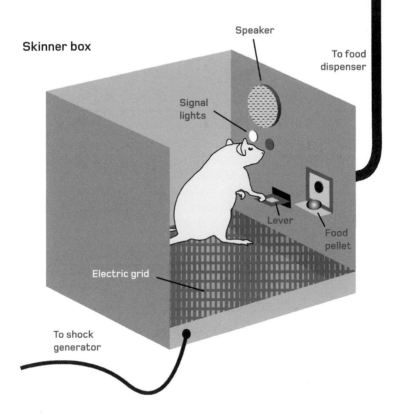

Skinner box

Speaker

Signal lights

To food dispenser

Lever

Food pellet

Electric grid

To shock generator

Animal experimentation

The joke that "psychology is the science of pulling habits out of rats" is based on the experimental methods of the behaviorists. With the exception of Watson's Little Albert experiment, behaviorist theories resulted from and were tested by experiments on animals. As well as the ubiquitous "lab rat," psychologists have used cats, dogs, and chicks, and Skinner latterly found pigeons ideal subjects for experiments.

Skinner, like most behaviorists, was opposed to human experimentation, but his ethics were questioned when he invented a "baby tender," a secure container with a controlled environment to be used as an alternative cot. It was satirized as a Skinner box for children and dubbed "the heir conditioner." Skinner believed that operant conditioning works in the same way for all organisms, and observation of any animal gives insights into human behavior. Although most behaviorists would have agreed, many other psychologists see animal experimentation of limited use in studying human psychology.

Skinner's teaching machine

Unlike classical conditioning, which explains how behavior can be shaped and controlled, operant conditioning offered an explanation of how animals learn through interaction with the external world. For Skinner, the emphasis was on learning, rather than teaching or training, and in his version of the stimulus-response model, the learner is an active participant, not merely a subject.

However, Skinner recognized the value of his idea of positive reinforcement to education. An inveterate tinkerer, he invented a "teaching machine" that allowed students to learn in stages, and gave positive feedback for correct answers in tests at the end of each stage. The same basic principle was later used for many interactive self-education computer learning programs. Skinner also developed a teaching program along the same lines, which was widely adopted in schools in the USA and elsewhere, with teachers encouraging their students by giving positive feedback at each stage of their courses.

Inside a Skinner teaching machine

When the lid is closed, the machine presents the student with a question and paper for their answer

Wheel holding preselected questions and answers for student to match up

Paper roll for student's answers

Lever for student to score answers and track progress

Rewards and punishments

In one respect, Skinner's observations brought about a complete change of direction in education. Previously, the emphasis had been on discipline to control behavior, and punishment not only for wrongdoing but also for wrong answers. Skinner had seen in experiments that negative reinforcement is weaker than positive reinforcement for encouragement of good behavior.

He advocated praise rather than a physical reward, and disapproved of physical punishment to discourage errant ways. Punishment, Skinner argued, not only is less effective than positive encouragement, but also negative reinforcement of any kind can even be counterproductive. Punishing someone for behaving in a certain way is not necessarily going to discourage them, especially if the behavior is pleasurable. But it might encourage them to modify their behavior to avoid punishment— for example, by continuing in secret. Withholding praise works as a negative reinforcement more effectively than punishment.

Imprinting

Skinner's "radical behaviorism" (see page 72) led him to believe that we have no free will, that our behavior is determined by the selection of actions with positive consequences and, moreover, our ability to operate on our environment is determined genetically.

In the 1930s, the naturalist Konrad Lorenz noticed that young geese formed an attachment to their mother immediately upon hatching, and could be persuaded to adopt almost any object as a "foster parent" if this was the first moving thing they saw. This behavior, which Lorenz called imprinting, is not learned but appears to be instinctive, permanent, and only happens at this very early stage in the chicks' lives. Lorenz later identified several other instinctive behaviors that emerge at different stages in animals' lives, which similarly are not learned by imitation or conditioning. He concluded that these "fixed-action patterns" of behavior are genetically determined and, as such, have evolved through natural selection.

Behaviorism vs. instinct

While Skinner had come to the conclusion that we have a genetically determined predisposition to learn behavior through operant conditioning, Lorenz went as far as to propose that at least some animal behavior is itself genetically programed. Other psychologists maintained that all behavior is learned and even—as Watson had proposed (see page 62)—that through conditioning anyone can be trained to do anything. Perhaps the most extreme advocate of this behaviorist approach was the Chinese psychologist Zing-Yang Kuo, who dismissed the notion of instinct as merely a convenient way to explain behavior that was not properly understood. He believed the aggression of cats toward rats, for example, was not instinctive but learned. In experiments he reared kittens and rats together and found that the cats did not act aggressively toward the rats but even treated them as playmates. He concluded that all animals undergo a process of ongoing development which shapes their behavior, and there is no such thing as innate or inherited behavior.

Cognitive psychology

The term "cognitive psychology" is nowadays associated with the approach to psychology that became predominant after the Second World War, focusing on mental processes rather than behavior. But from the earliest days of psychology as a scientific discipline, psychologists had set out to study the way our minds work.

Although behaviorism, which dismissed cognitive processes as unobservable and irrelevant, dominated psychology in the USA, German psychologists continued to explore ways of examining these mental activities. Hermann Ebbinghaus and Wilhelm Wundt laid the foundations for a scientific study of memory and perception, and later, Gestalt psychology (see page 110) provided a comprehensive explanation of mental processes that countered behaviorism's emphasis on conditioning. Cognitive psychology formally emerged in the 1950s, with the so-called "cognitive revolution"—a movement largely influenced by advances in information and computer sciences.

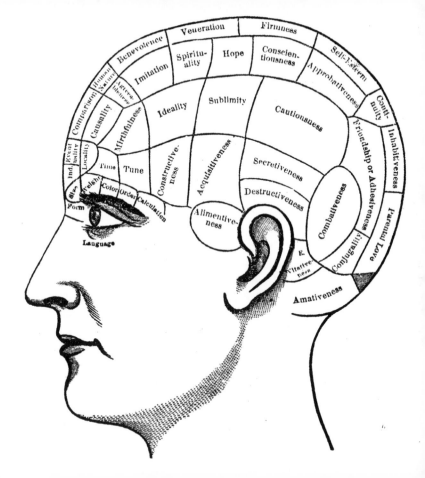

Memory

One of the pioneers of the scientific study of memory was the German psychologist Hermann Ebbinghaus, who in the late 19th century examined his own ability to remember lists of words and letters, making a note of how well and for how long he retained the information. From his observations, he identified patterns of how we learn and forget, and his discoveries laid the foundations for the study of memory to the present day. His methods, however, were less influential.

Although he was meticulous in the design of his experiments and went about them systematically, Ebbinghaus used no other subject than himself. As we cannot have direct access to what is going on in other people's minds, he believed that mental processes could only be studied by introspection. Other experimental psychologists viewed this approach as subjective and unscientific, and went onto devise other experimental techniques for studying cognitive processes with several different subjects.

Memorizing and recalling

In the 1880s, Hermann Ebbinghaus set out to examine the ways in which we commit things to memory, and what factors affect how well we have memorized them. To do this, he devised a number of memory tasks for himself, such as memorizing lists of words, and tested his ability to recall them later. He systematically organized his experiments so that he could measure and record the effectiveness of learning a list in a specific time frame—not only at one sitting, but also in separate sessions at various intervals of time—checking his recall after various time periods.

Ebbinghaus' experiments recognized the two distinct processes of memorization and recall, with recall being an effective measure of learning efficiency. In this way, he could compare the results of the different "schedules" of memorizing and the effect of time on his ability to recall information. As well as discovering patterns in the way we remember things, he discovered there is also a pattern to the way we forget.

Forgetting

One of the things Ebbinghaus discovered would come as no surprise to any student who has tried "cramming" the day before an exam: 24 hours after learning something, we forget about two-thirds of it. But he found that there are ways of overcoming this rapid, exponential "forgetting curve." He noticed that information sticks in our memory better if learned over several sessions, and that things that are repeatedly recalled are more easily retrieved from memory.

As well as lists of words, Ebbinghaus tested his ability to learn lists of three-letter nonsense syllables. He found that he scored much lower when trying to recall these than words that had meaning, and concluded that memorizing and recalling information is more efficient if it is meaningful. Our minds do not simply store and retrieve information mechanically, but go through a cognitive process of trying to make sense of it, so that important or significant information is more efficiently stored and more easily retrieved.

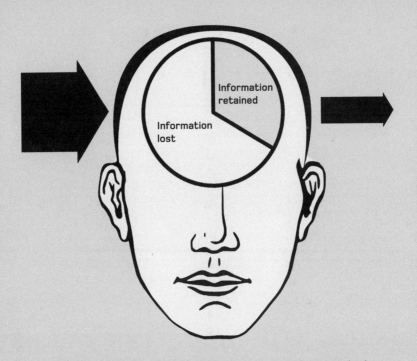

Ebbinghaus estimated that over a 24-hour period, about two-thirds of information is lost.

The Zeigarnik effect

Ebbinghaus identified distinct patterns of memory and forgetting from the results of his experiments. As well as rapid onset and slow decline that marks what he called the forgetting curve, he noticed a similar "learning curve" associated with memorizing. When we learn a list of things, for instance, we tend to remember the items at the beginning and the end, better than those in the middle of the list.

The Russian psychologist Bluma Zeigarnik later discovered another distinctive feature of memory, when watching waiters in her local café. If asked about what someone had ordered, they could remember the order exactly if it had not yet been paid for, but found it much more difficult to recall once the check had been settled. Memory of a completed transaction was no longer important and was "put to one side" to make room for new orders. In later experiments, Zeigarnik found that an unfinished or interrupted task tends to be better remembered than one that has been completed.

Long-term and short-term memory

As psychologists applied a methodical approach to studying memory, it became clear that it is not just a simple matter of storing and retrieving information. There appear to be two different kinds of memory store: short-term memory (STM) and long-term memory (LTM). STM holds information for only a matter of seconds and has a limited capacity, while LTM can store unlimited amounts of information indefinitely.

STM deals with the information we need to use immediately, but anything that needs to be remembered for future use is stored in LTM. For example, when we look up a phone number, our STM remembers it just long enough for us to dial the number. But if it is a number we are going to need later, or that we use repeatedly, we memorize it by moving it into LTM. Most psychologists recognize this dual-store model of memory, but there is some disagreement as to the exact roles of STM and LTM, their connection and whether they are in fact separate systems.

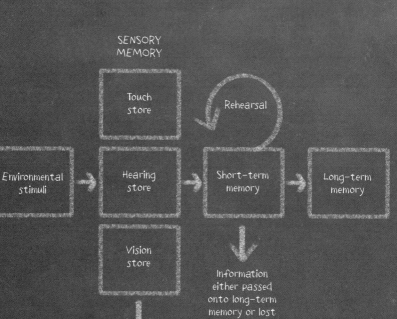

A model of how sensory memories are processed and long-term memories formed.

"Assemblies" of brain cells

The concept of "storage" of memory gave rise to the idea that there is a physical place in our brains where memories are stored, or at least, that memory—like other mental processes—is located in a specific area of the brain. In the 1940s, however, Karl Lashley showed that memory is not associated with any particular part of the brain, but is evenly distributed across the whole brain. Lashley's colleague, Donald Hebb, went onto describe the way we learn in terms of neural connections.

Every action or experience sets up a distinct pattern of connections. Hebb explained, "cells that fire together, wire together"—if the action or experience is repeated, connections are strengthened and become "hardwired" in our brains as "assemblies" of cells. We learn by making associations between different assemblies—for example, when a baby learns to associate the sound of its mother coming with the idea of seeing her face and being picked up.

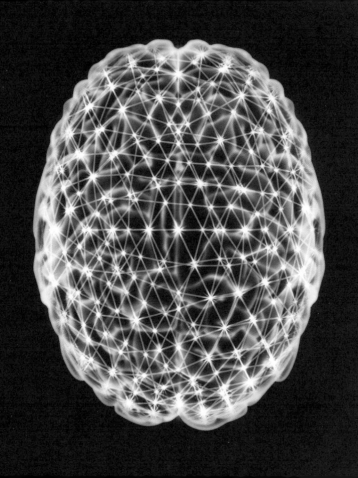

Learning language

Until the 1950s, our understanding of how we learn was based almost entirely on behaviorist theories of the stimulus–response model of conditioning. Not all psychologists were convinced, however, and beginning in 1955, American Noam Chomsky presented an alternative explanation of learning. In it, he showed that as we learn language, we need to make sense of it, rather than simply learning "parrot fashion."

Chomsky noticed that children progress much faster in learning language than they would by simply imitating, and have a grasp of complex grammatical structures at a very young age. He concluded that all languages have a similar underlying structure—a "universal grammar"—and that we have an innate ability to use this to find meaning as we learn language. Chomsky's theory of language learning is sometimes said to have sparked a "cognitive revolution" in psychology, shifting emphasis from behavior to mental processes—but for many European psychologists the approach was nothing new.

Language learning is believed to be a cognitive process and not a form of conditioning.

Problem-solving

Behaviorist psychologists in the USA had been influenced by Pavlov's experiments and tended to study animal behavior in terms of stimulus and response. The German psychologist Wolfgang Köhler, however, felt that the approach missed a lot. Köhler was a cofounder of the Gestalt movement (see page 110), and spent several years as director of a research center on Tenerife observing a chimpanzee colony.

Setting them tasks and watching the way in which they went about solving them, he noticed that they did not use a simple process of trial and error. After trying unsuccessfully to solve a problem, such as getting food from a high or inaccessible place, a chimp would pause and think until it came up with a different method, often using a stick or climbing on a box. If the solution worked, it was used again for similar problems. Köhler realized that, rather than physical trial and error, the chimp went over the problem in its mind, learning by a cognitive process of perception and insight.

Perception

While we are awake, our sensory organs provide us with a huge amount of information, from which we can make an inner representation of the external world. Instead of experiencing this sensory information simply as sensation, our minds organize and interpret what our senses tell us. This is the cognitive process we know as perception. In order to interact with the world, we need to make sense of what we see, hear, touch, smell, and taste, and to distinguish between what is important and what is irrelevant.

Perception is our ability to distinguish foreground from background, for example, and also identify objects and their position. Most of the time, we do this without consciously thinking about it. Some psychologists—especially those in the Gestalt movement—believe that this ability is somehow hardwired into our brains, that we are "programed" to organize the information into meaningful forms. Others believe that perception is something we learn from experience.

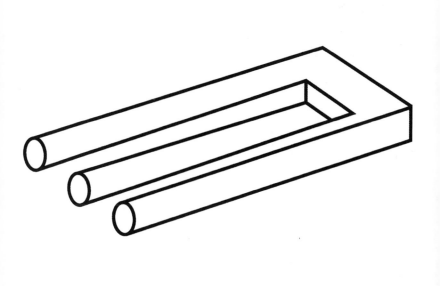

Gestalt psychology

At the turn of the 20th century, a group of German psychologists proposed a different way of looking at cognition and perception. Rather than the prevalent "structuralism" of psychologists such as Wilhelm Wundt, who sought to identify the separate elements of each mental process, they suggested a more holistic approach. It took its name from the German word *gestalt*, meaning "form, shape, or essence." Gestalt psychology emerged from the work of Wolfgang Köhler, Max Wertheimer, and Kurt Koffka.

According to Gestalt theory, we have an inbuilt tendency to perceive an object as a meaningful whole, rather than piecing together the form of the object from its separate parts. For example, when we see a simple drawing of a square, we perceive the shape as a whole, not four separate lines, and when we see a particular sequence of flashing lights, we perceive that as motion. As Koffka put it, "The whole is different from the sum of its parts."

The individual parts of a clock signify very little separately. Gestalt psychologists maintain that we understand objects as a meaningful whole rather than as the sum of their parts.

The Gestalt laws of perception

At the heart of Gestalt theory is the idea that our minds interpret sensory information in regular and predictable ways following certain "rules." These so-called Gestalt laws of perception are more like descriptions of mental shortcuts that allow us to perceive things quickly without consciously having to process vast amounts of information.

The concept of *Prägnanz*—meaning "conciseness" or "simplicity"—encapsulates the principle that underlies these laws: we perceive objects in a way that makes them appear as simple as possible. Looking at the Olympics logo, for example, we immediately see five rings, and not a collection of complicated shapes and lines. From this general rule others are derived: the law of similarity—we group similar objects; the law of proximity—we group things that are close to each other; the law of continuity—we perceive things in smooth lines as connected; and the law of closure—we fill in gaps in information, grouping things that look like parts of a single object.

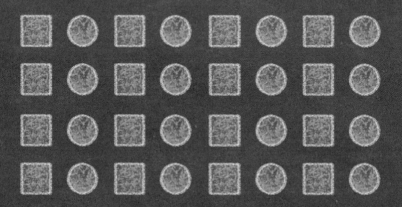

Law of similarity: the human brain instantly perceives groups of similar shapes—in this case, vertical columns of squares and circles.

Pattern recognition

Gestalt psychologists were not the first to employ the psychological concept of Gestalt. In the 1890s, the philosopher Christian von Ehrenfels described Gestalt as an emergent property of a perceived object, a secondary quality that emerges from connections between its component parts —the exact opposite of the principle of Gestalt psychology.

Although Gestalt theory was attractive and influential, it has been criticized for merely describing and not explaining the cognitive process of perception. Later psychologists returned to the idea that we identify objects by recognizing patterns in their component parts. Theories of pattern recognition are based on the notion that our memory stores a set of "object templates," which we compare with incoming sensory information. Irving Biederman introduced such a set of simple geometric figures, called "geons" (geometric icons). Another theory involves feature detection—the visual ability to scan a scene and pick out recognizable features.

Geons   Objects composed of geons

Recognizing faces

Theories that say visual perception is a process of pattern recognition are supported by the everyday experience of seeing shapes and patterns in clouds, rocks, and natural formations. We seem particularly attuned to picking out facial features—the Man in the Moon, for example, is a special case of pattern recognition.

There is evidence to suggest that our ability to identify faces is innate. Our brains are hardwired to distinguish facial patterns from all other incoming visual information, and it is certainly something that we can do from a very early age. But as well as being able to pick out faces from a background, we can detect even small differences in their features, enabling us to recognize different people at a glance without needing to analyze the individual features of each face. What's more, humans are expert at detecting patterns in the component features, such as the shape of a mouth or eyes, that allow us to interpret a person's emotional state.

Processing information

Even though many European psychologists had studied mental processes, cognitive psychology as an alternative approach to behaviorism did not emerge until after the Second World War. Wartime advances in computers and information technology provided psychologists with a model for cognitive processes as a kind of information processing. Perception and memory could be explained as the way that our minds classify and organize incoming information, but so could learning, providing a counter to the behaviorist idea of conditioning. The American psychologist Jerome Bruner, who founded the Center for Cognitive Studies at Harvard with George Armitage Miller, was among the first to describe learning as a cognitive process. He held that in order to learn we need to make sense of information by active participation. With the emphasis on cognition as a form of information processing, cognitive psychologists revived interest in the processes of memory and perception as well as learning. In Britain, Donald Broadbent and others explored the new field of attention.

The magical number 7

At the forefront of the "cognitive revolution" in psychology in the USA was George Armitage Miller who, more than others, adopted the information-processing model. His best-known contribution was in the area of memory and in particular the workings of short-term memory (STM). Ebbinghaus and others had long before identified a memory of short duration and limited capacity through which information passes before being stored in long-term memory (LTM—see page 100).

Miller famously (with tongue-in-cheek) quantified the capacity of STM as seven items in an article titled "The Magical Number Seven, Plus or Minus Two." More importantly, he interpreted STM as an information-processing phenomenon, a kind of filter that determines what is stored in LTM. From this idea, others, notably Alan Baddeley and Graham Hitch, developed the notion of a "working memory." Under the control of a "central executive," working memory sorts out which information needs its attention and what of that is to be passed onto LTM.

Chunking

Because of the limited capacity of STM, we can only memorize a finite amount of information at any one time —Miller's "magical" seven items. Given the large amount of incoming information from our senses, there is the potential for an information bottleneck. Only a small percentage of the information, however, is passed from "sensory memory" to STM.

Miller also discovered that the capacity of STM can be extended by organizing new information into "chunks" of related items. If we assume STM has seven "ports," then a list of more than seven items overloads the system. But if, for example, a string of letters has a particular sequence (R, S, T, U, V, W, X, Y, Z) or forms a recognizable word (MEMORIZING), our STM can deal with it this as a single item, leaving capacity for other information. Similarly, the 14-digit string 11235813213455 is not at all memorable, but once we realize it is in fact the first ten numbers of the Fibonacci sequence, it is turned into one "chunk" to process.

120007041776

=

noon (1200)

July 4th (0704)

1776

Attention

The British psychologist Donald Broadbent, like his contemporary George Miller, adopted a model of the mind as information processor in the 1950s. He, too, realized that there is much more incoming sensory information than our minds can consciously deal with, just as STM has a limited capacity. Rather than memory, however, Broadbent approached the problem from the perspective of attention—how we allocate our limited resources for processing that information.

He likened the mind to a radio receiving many channels at the same time. In order to cope with this, it has to select the most important feed and concentrate on that, tuning out the other channels. More recently, the selective nature of our limited ability to process information was dramatically illustrated by the "invisible gorilla" experiments. Told to count the number of times a basketball is passed from player to player in a video, participants completely failed to notice a person in a gorilla suit crossing the scene and waving to the camera.

The cocktail party problem

Donald Broadbent's analysis of attention as a means of allocating our limited capacity for processing incoming information was similar to studies conducted in communications science in the years following the Second World War. The "cocktail party effect," identified by information scientist Colin Cherry, recognizes how we focus on a single conversation at a party, selectively "tuning out" several others that are happening simultaneously as well as the blaring music.

His findings mirrored those of Broadbent's dichotic listening experiments, in which participants wearing headphones received different information in each ear, leading Broadbent to conclude that we can only listen to one voice at a time. When faced with a number of "channels" of incoming information, our minds can only concentrate on one. We therefore focus our attention selectively on the channel that our mind determines is most important, and filter out what it considers to be background noise.

Filter models

Broadbent explained the way we focus attention on a particular "channel" of information as a kind of selective filter. Our minds select which channel it is that we need to attend to, and process all incoming information according to characteristics, such as pitch, loudness, direction, color, and so on, filtering out any that do not match those properties. He found in his studies, however, that the meaning of the

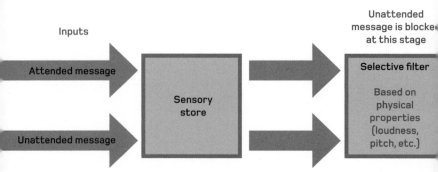

Inputs

Attended message

Unattended message

Sensory store

Unattended message is blocked at this stage

Selective filter

Based on physical properties (loudness, pitch, etc.)

information also played a part in the filtering process. For example, pilots switch their attention from one channel to another if an urgent message comes through. Colin Cherry had also noticed something similar in his study of the cocktail party effect (see page 126)—even though someone is concentrating on a conversation, if he or she hears his or her name mentioned in another conversation it is impossible to maintain focus. This suggests that even when we are actively focusing on one "info feed," we hear and can distinguish meaning in at least some of the information that is filtered out. The filter helps us to detect what is important out of all the information competing for our attention.

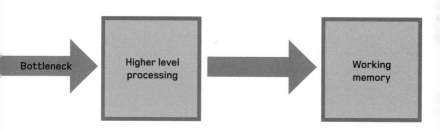

Different kinds
of memory

Memory continued to figure in cognitive psychology in the 1970s, especially with the pioneering work of the Estonian-Canadian psychologist Endel Tulving. But while cognitive psychologists had previously focused on the differences between STM and LTM, Tulving took a much broader approach. Returning to Ebbinghaus' ideas (see pages 92–97), he showed that memory consists of two distinct but related mental processes: memorizing, or storing information; and recall, or retrieving information from storage.

Tulving also identified three basic kinds of memory: episodic, or memories of events and experiences; semantic, or memories of facts and knowledge; and procedural, or memories of how to do things. Our minds organize information according to type and put it into different kinds of memory store, which are further subdivided into "categories." When we need to retrieve information, rather than having to search the whole "memory bank," our minds can narrow the field by category.

Recalling memories

Cognitive psychology's approach to the study of memory was largely based on the analogy of information storage and retrieval, and the connection between the two processes. Endel Tulving explained memories as being organized by our minds into categories, which are put into different stores, and showed that these could be recalled by "jogging the memory" with a cue.

He also described remembering as a form of "mental time travel," taking us back to the time and circumstances when the memory was stored. This idea was taken up by British psychologist Alan Baddeley, who showed that divers recalled things better in the circumstances in which they had been learned. Gordon H. Bower discovered that our memories are not only cue-dependent but also mood-dependent—our feelings when storing and retrieving memories affect their recall. When we are in a bad mood, for instance, it is easier to remember unhappy memories than good times.

Memories can be strongly linked—many people remember where they were and even what they were doing when they heard that Elvis had died.

Seven sins of memory

It is remarkable how much we remember, but inevitably our recall can let us down. When trying to retrieve information from memory storage, there are a number of ways things can go wrong—what Daniel Schacter calls the "seven sins of memory." This may be the fault of transience: that memories fade with time especially if they are not accessed regularly. Absentmindedness is caused by faulty storage, perhaps because we were not concentrating at the time of storing the memory, allowing our minds to "categorize" the information as unimportant. The sin of blocking is when we cannot retrieve a memory because another is getting in its way, leading to "tip of the tongue" syndrome. At other times, the retrieval process is faulty, so we recall the information correctly but misattribute its source. Our memories can also be distorted by the cues that trigger the recollection (suggestibility), or the thoughts and feelings we have at the time we recall it (bias). The sin of persistence, by contrast, makes it impossible to get rid of a memory.

transience

absentmindedness

blocking

misattribution

suggestibility

bias

persistence

Unreliable memories

What Schacter called the "sin of suggestibility" has particular relevance in the legal world. Court cases often rely heavily on evidence from victims and eyewitnesses, but our memory of events is less than rock solid. American psychologist Elizabeth Loftus showed in experiments how leading questions can influence recollection. Participants were shown a movie of two cars colliding and their estimates of the vehicles' speed varied depending on whether they were described as "bumping" or "crashing" into each other.

Loftus also demonstrated that memories of traumatic events are especially susceptible. More worryingly, she showed that it is possible to have a memory of something that never happened, in an experiment where participants were led to believe they had been lost in a shopping mall as a child. This kind of "false memory" calls into question the reliability of witness evidence, and casts doubt on the validity of Freud's theory about the effects of repressed memories (see page 152).

Illusions and paradoxes

Just as our memories sometimes mislead us, so does our perception, especially our ability to visually make sense of the three-dimensional world. Even when we look at a 2D representation of a scene, our minds interpret visual clues to pinpoint the relative positions of things. We can tell whether one object is behind another by the way edges overlap and relative sizes of familiar objects, and parallel lines converging toward a vanishing point give us a sense of perspective. But our minds are easily tricked by optical illusions.

In the 1950s, Roger Shepard, a psychologist and deviser of aural and visual illusions, explained that our ability to make sense of the world comes from experience—we mentally compare what we see with our past experiences and interpret it according to our expectations. But J.J. Gibson disputed this two-step process, saying that it is a single process of direct perception: our minds might be deceived by 2D images of 3D objects, but we rarely make the same mistakes in the real world.

Decision making

Humans' ability to reason and make rational decisions is popularly considered as the most important of our mental processes. Yet it received comparatively little attention from psychologists until the 1970s. While their contemporaries examined ways in which memory and perception sometimes let us down, Daniel Kahneman and Amos Tversky investigated why, with our mental capacities, we should so often make errors.

They concluded that although we have the ability to think about a problem before making a decision, instead we often rely on "heuristics," or rules of thumb, based on past experience. This is partly because we may not have the time to weigh up all the pros and cons, and also because our minds are "lazy" and prefer the easy option. We have two decision-making systems—fast and slow—and we regularly fall back on fast thinking. The snag is that this system is often susceptible to errors of cognitive bias—previous experience is all too often based on small, unrepresentative samples and subject to personal prejudices.

Psychoanalysis and psychodynamics

At the end of the 19th century a different approach to psychology was evolving from the medical treatment of mental disorders. At the forefront of this new branch of psychology was the Viennese neurologist Sigmund Freud. He proposed an alternative approach to psychopathology based on his description of the structure of the mind and treatment by talking with a trained therapist. Freud believed that the dynamic relationship between the conscious and unconscious is the key factor in human behavior. Drawing parallels with energy in thermodynamic systems, the term "psychodynamic," referring to psychic energy, is sometimes used to describe this approach. Freud's theories of the mind and the relationship between its constituent parts, along with the method of psychoanalysis he developed to diagnose and treat mental disorders, were enormously influential. The psychodynamic model was adopted and refined by Carl Jung (see page 160), Alfred Adler (see page 164), and others, paving the way for the "talking cures" of psychotherapy (see page 144).

The talking cure

Freud used hypnosis (see page 14) in his treatment of patients in his private neurology practice in Vienna, and the idea of a "talking cure" grew from this. His colleague, Josef Breuer, first noted the beneficial effects of a patient simply talking about his or her disorder with a therapist without the need for hypnotic suggestion. It was one of his patients, Anna O' (Bertha Pappenheim), who coined the term "talking cure."

Freud adopted the method and found that many of the symptoms of psychological disorders were alleviated by exploring the thoughts and feelings of the patient. In sessions with patients suffering from "hysteria" and "neurosis" (now classed as anxiety disorders), he developed the idea that these and many other mental disorders have their roots in inner conflict, especially between the conscious and the unconscious mind. Freud believed talking can help to identify and resolve this conflict, but could be more effective if the therapist had an understanding of the structure of the human mind.

The unconscious

Freud's "talking cure" of the 1890s led him to develop a comprehensive theory of the way the human mind is structured. He realized that what we are consciously thinking is only a fraction of what is going on in our minds. Beneath the superficial level of the conscious mind, there is the preconscious, Freud proposed, containing thoughts and memories that we can easily access. Further below is a much larger unconscious, where he believed repressed thoughts, memories, and feelings are stored. As well as these horizontal divisions of the mind, Freud later identified three separate parts of the psyche—the id, the ego, and the superego. The id is the childlike part of our selves that works on the "pleasure principle," seeking immediate gratification of basic impulses. The ego embodies the adult "reality principle," the voice of reason moderating and supervising the id. Thirdly, the superego is the "judging principle," the voice of morality imposed upon us by our parents and society. Conflict between these opposing "voices" is the root cause of many psychological problems.

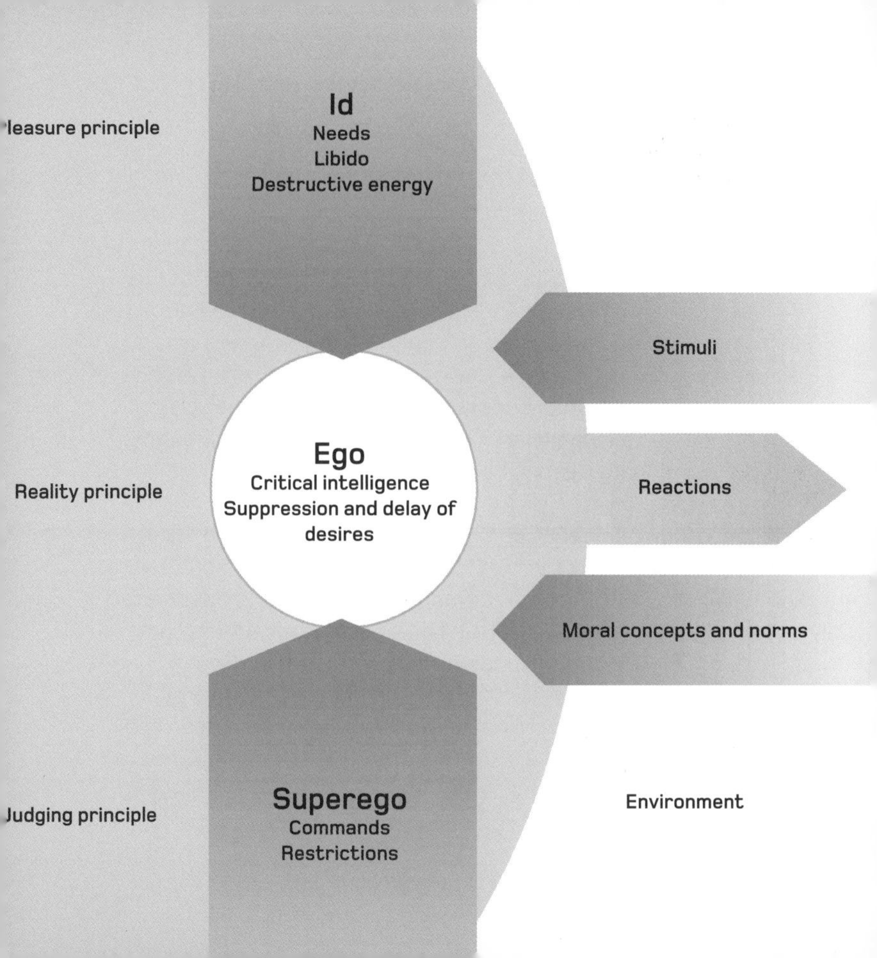

Id
Needs
Libido
Destructive energy

Pleasure principle

Stimuli

Ego
Critical intelligence
Suppression and delay of
desires

Reality principle

Reactions

Moral concepts and norms

Superego
Commands
Restrictions

Judging principle

Environment

Drives

A prevalent 19th-century belief was the notion of "psychic energy," which lies behind our motivation to behave in certain ways. Freud believed not only in the existence of this psychic force, but also that it remained powerful even when pushed out of our conscious minds. He believed that it continues to exert an influence on our conscious thoughts and behavior from deep in the unconscious.

The fundamental energy comes from our "lust for life," which manifests itself in instinctive drives for such things as food and drink, sex, intimacy, and companionship. As it is associated with the pleasure principle, it is the energy that drives the id, the only wholly unconscious component of the psyche. The hedonistic impulses prompted by this psychic energy may come into conflict with the moderating influence of the ego and superego. Freud later identified an opposing form of psychic energy, what he called "death drives"—impulses for self-destruction and an urge to return to an inanimate state.

Freud theorized that human nature emerged out of two basic drives—Eros, the instinct for life and sexuality, and Thanatos, the desire for death.

Psychosexual stages of development

A significant part of the positive "psychic energy" of the id is the libido, or drive for sexual pleasure. Freud believed this is an innate drive, affecting us differently in various stages of development. He believed the libido is centered on a different part of the body at each stage of development. In the first stage, the oral stage, the focus is on the mouth as the infant seeks and derives pleasure from feeding. Next, the focus shifts in the anal stage, as the child derives pleasure from learning to control bowel and bladder.

In the phallic stage, from about three to six years of age, the child discovers the pleasures of the genitals and gender differences. This is followed by what Freud called a stage of latency when the libido is dormant, until a fully mature genital stage reemerges in puberty. Frustration of the libido by parental or societal disapproval (at any stage) leads to fixation on the associated erogenous zone—for example, the obsessively ordered behavior we would call "anally retentive."

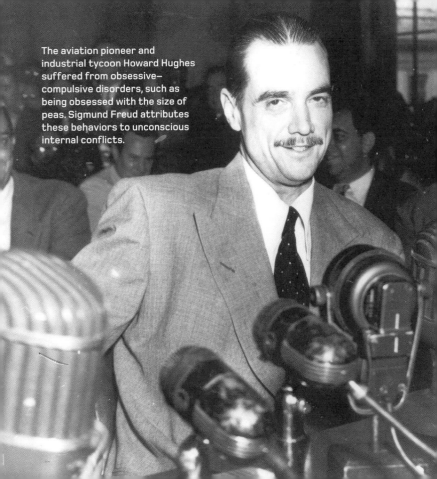

The aviation pioneer and industrial tycoon Howard Hughes suffered from obsessive–compulsive disorders, such as being obsessed with the size of peas. Sigmund Freud attributes these behaviors to unconscious internal conflicts.

Repression

Freud explained that frustration of the libido at crucial stages of development causes anxiety that persists into adult life, not just as sexual problems but also in the form of hysteria or neurosis. The reasons for this frustration are often because the hedonism of libido goes against cultural norms, and a child may be made to feel shame for his or her pleasures.

Freud also recognized that this was not the only cause of conflict within the psyche. Anything that is unacceptable to the conscious is repressed, pushed down into the unconscious. Powerful emotions, such as fear, shame, horror, and anger, are often unbearable, and are consigned to the unconscious. Traumatic and terrifying memories, such as childhood abuse, are repressed. So too are ideas and desires our conscious considers unacceptable, such as sexual attraction to a "forbidden" person or the irrational wish to kill someone. We may not be aware of them, but these repressed thoughts, feelings, and memories set up internal conflicts that influence our conscious minds.

Analysis

In order to treat the psychological disorders caused by conflict between the unconscious and conscious mind, Freud developed techniques to access the repressed thoughts, memories, and feelings in the unconscious, and subject them to a process of analysis. For the psychoanalyst, the unconscious consists of what has been repressed because it is unacceptable to the conscious mind, and the patient is therefore reluctant to reveal its contents.

Initially, Freud and others used hypnosis in an attempt to access the unconscious, but later found techniques such as free association and dream interpretation useful ways to uncover unconscious thoughts. In the process of psychoanalysis, therapist and patient explore the memories and thoughts lurking in the unconscious, identifying those repressed ideas that are most powerful. Then, they are subjected to scrutiny, bringing to light the hidden causes of the psychological conflict with the conscious and resolving them.

Free association

It was Josef Breuer's patient, Anna O, who coined the term "talking cure" and arguably first introduced the idea of free association in psychoanalysis. She explained that it helped to relieve her symptoms if she was allowed to talk freely without concentrating on anything in particular. Freud picked up on this technique, recognizing that when giving free rein to their thoughts, people often unwittingly reveal things hidden in their unconscious—an effect popularly known as a "Freudian slip."

As well as simply letting his patients talk freely, Freud guided this process of association by asking them to respond without thinking to a word or phrase, which could sometimes offer an insight into unconscious thoughts. He noticed that in many cases another association was made—his patients often directed at him, the therapist, feelings and ideas they had about other significant figures in their lives. This process of "transference" also offered an opportunity to explore repressed thoughts.

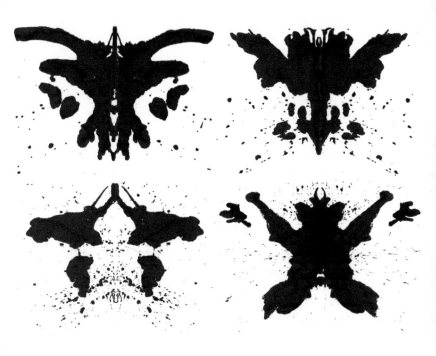

Utilizing free association to identify the shapes, the ten cards of the Rorschach inkblot test can be a starting point for a conversation about a patient's internal world.

Dreams and dream analysis

When we are asleep we have little or no contact with the external world and our conscious mind is inactive. Our dreams, therefore, are purely a product of our unconscious and can give us access to it. Freud described dreams as the "royal road to the unconscious," and along with free association, it was a cornerstone of his psychoanalysis technique.

He saw dreams as a sort of wish fulfillment. Because we are not inhibited by conscious reason or cultural norms in dreams, we can do what we like—what our unconscious really wants but our conscious is repressing. Even so, our dreams often seem random or meaningless. Here, it is the analyst's task to help the patient interpret his or her dreams by sorting out the true, latent meaning from the superficial manifest content. Dream analysis also featured largely in the psychoanalysis of Freud's student Carl Jung (see page 160), who took his teacher's ideas further. Jung believed that dreams contain a wealth of symbols representing aspect of the psyche that require interpretation.

Sleep is when the unconscious mind comes out to play. Jung believed that the demons and visions released by sleep are the keys to the unconscious.

The collective unconscious

Freud's most brilliant student, Carl Jung, soon found fault with many of his teacher's theories about the unconscious. Jung's model for the structure of the psyche, for example, was divided into the ego, the personal unconscious, and the collective unconscious. The ego represented immediate consciousness, and the personal unconscious was the store for all personal experiences, both forgotten or repressed. The collective unconscious, however, is a separate psychic system, which does not develop from our experience but is inherited.

The idea of a collective consciousness grew as Jung noticed recurrent and strikingly similar ideas, myths, and symbols that appear in folk tales, literature, and art of all cultures. These, he concluded, were manifestations of forms, or archetypes, that are innate and exist identically in every individual's unconscious. Whether this is simply a genetic predisposition, according to which the human species must experience the universe, or a reference to an inclusive "world-soul" is open to debate.

Archetypes

According to Jung, the symbols, characters, and myths that are common to all human cultures derive from concepts we each have in our collective unconscious. We have an innate tendency to use these "archetypes," as he called them, to understand and interpret the world by translating them into recognizable archetypal images. Whole stories, such as the myth of the flood, are based on archetypal motifs, as are rituals surrounding rites of passage.

Many familiar characters, such as the Wise Old Man, the Goddess, the Mother, the Child, the Hero, or the Trickster can be identified as archetypal figures. Archetypes also help us to understand our personalities: the Persona represents our public image, in contrast to the True Self and the Shadow, the things we hide from others and project onto them. The Animus (male) and Anima (female) are the complementary "other half" of our gender personality, and give us an insight into the nature of the opposite sex.

Inferiority complex

Alfred Adler was for a time one of the most influential of Freud's students, presenting an alternative model of psychoanalysis, which he called "Individual psychology." Rather than analyzing the separate parts of the psyche, he considered the individual as an indivisible whole, placing greater emphasis on external factors on the individual than inner conflicts.

He is best known for stressing the importance of feelings of inferiority as a root cause of neurosis, the so-called inferiority complex. Adler's theory was that children's natural vulnerability makes them feel inferior to adults and older siblings, and has the positive effect of motivating them to achieve. In later life, the same feelings can prompt a person to compensate for shortcomings, and success brings a feeling of achievement and confidence in a balanced person. Some react to feelings of inferiority with resignation, and fail to achieve success or satisfaction, while others overcompensate with obsessive, unsatisfiable attempts to overcome their inferiority.

Psychoanalysis and children

Although Freud's psychodynamic theories stressed the importance of early stages of development in neuroses, it was not until the following generation that his psychoanalytic techniques were first used on children. Melanie Klein's work with very young children led to ideas that contradicted some of Freud's assumptions, particularly about the development of the superego, which Klein concluded is innate.

Klein believed that psychodynamic conflicts begin in the very earliest stage of life, when an infant's sexual drive is centered on the oral satisfaction of feeding. A child's interaction with its mother at this stage is decisive—the child's drives could be a "part-object" (the breast), or "whole-object" (the mother as a person). A powerful emotional conflict arises as the child recognizes its mother is more than simply an organ to feed it. Freud's daughter Anna, another pioneer of child analysis, rejected Klein's theories, defending her father's ideas, and driving a wedge between Kleinian and Freudian approaches.

The split between Freudian psychology, with its emphasis on psychosexual drives, and Kleinian theories continues today.

True Self and False Self

Donald Winnicott, a pediatrician who later trained as a psychoanalyst, followed in Melanie Klein's footsteps in applying the principles of psychoanalysis to child development. He developed the concept of the "True Self," the aspect of the psyche that allows us to live authentically and spontaneously, to form relationships and be creative, and generally feel alive.

According to Winnicott, the True Self develops from the relationship between a baby and its primary caregiver. A "good enough" parent prevents a child being traumatized by the realization of its vulnerability, and allows it to satisfy its curiosity with confidence. The "False Self" is a kind of protective mask, which later develops into compliant and conventional behavior. Winnicott is perhaps best known for identifying children's "security blankets" or favorite cuddly toys as transitional objects. In between being completely dependent on its mother and discovering its own independence, a child uses a transitional object in place of the bond between them.

Humanistic psychoanalysis

The humanistic psychology of Abraham Maslow and Carl Rogers (see pages 174–177) influenced psychoanalytic practice in a way that would distance it from its Freudian roots. Maslow's identification of psychological needs beyond the primitive drives described by Freud prompted a shift toward analysis as a means of enabling people to realize their potential.

The movement started with psychoanalyst Karen Horney's recognition of the pressure to conform to societal norms. She called it the tyranny of the "should," which sets up a conflict between the authentic wishes of a "real self" and the demands of an "ideal self." The idea was taken up by Erich Fromm, who said that much of the anxiety and hopelessness we feel comes from a sense of dissatisfaction with life arising from seeking comfort and pleasure from outside, rather than from within. This can be overcome by reacting rationally and openly to changing circumstances, and rediscovering our own unique abilities and ideas to connect authentically with other people and the world.

A genuine sense of satisfaction can be achieved by doing something for oneself, rather than seeking satisfaction from outside and the approval of others.

A meaning in life

Different interpretations of Freud's theories of the unconscious emerged in the 50 years after he first introduced the idea of psychoanalysis, but it wasn't until after the Second World War that some of his basic ideas were challenged. At the heart of Freudian psychodynamics is the "pleasure principle," the drive for basic pleasures that comes into conflict with the moderating influence of the ego and superego. Humanist psychologists, such as Maslow (see pages 44 and 354) pointed out that humans are motivated by more than just primitive urges. The Viennese psychiatrist Viktor Frankl, who experienced almost intolerable suffering as a Jew in a concentration camp, even questioned the "will to pleasure" as our primary motivation, saying instead that we are driven by a "will to meaning"—the most important thing is finding meaning in life. We have the freedom to decide for ourselves how circumstances affect us and can choose to interpret events so that they have a meaning for us. In this way, even suffering can become endurable if it can be shown to be meaningful.

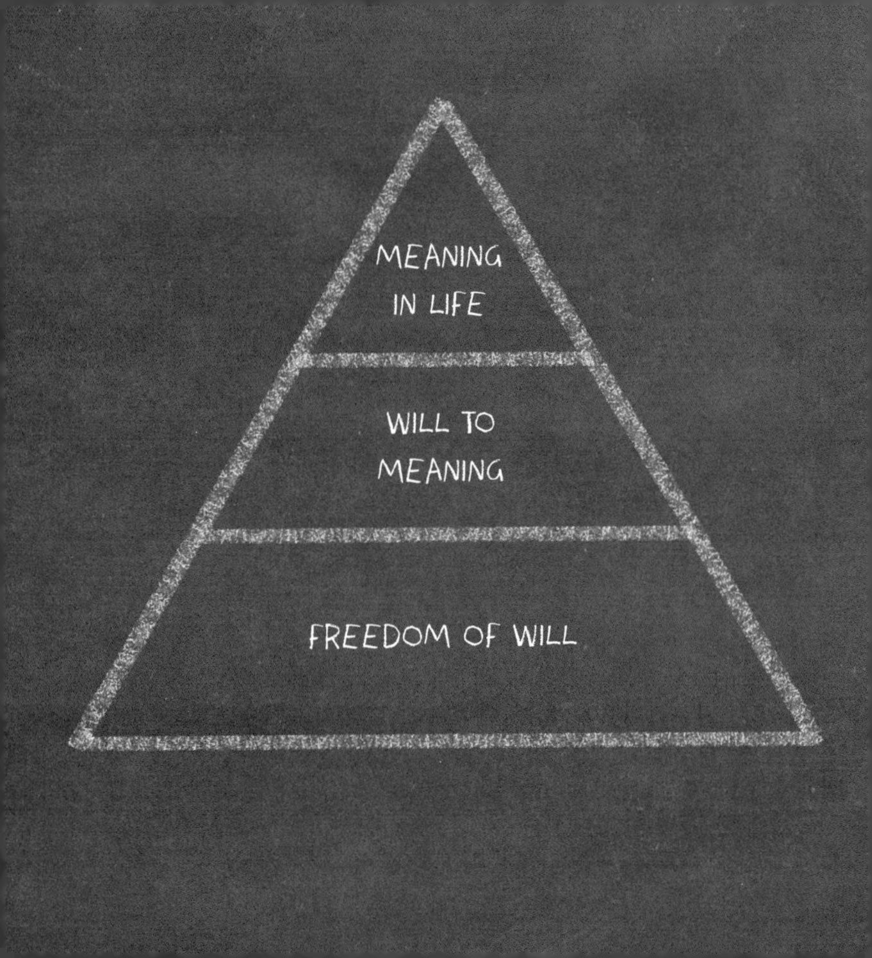
MEANING
IN LIFE
WILL TO
MEANING
FREEDOM OF WILL

Existential psychotherapy

Like all living creatures, humans have a natural tendency to seek pleasure and avoid pain. Seeking of pleasure is a fundamental principle of Freudian psychoanalytical theory, but existential philosophers including Søren Kierkegaard, Friedrich Nietzsche (pictured), and Martin Heidegger pointed out that this does not reflect our experience of the real world, and we must take personal responsibility for every aspect of our existence.

One of the first to apply the principles of existentialism to psychoanalysis was the American psychologist Rollo May, who was also influenced by Abraham Maslow's humanist psychology. Anxiety, May suggested, is a normal part of human existence, as are other forms of suffering. It is repression of our negative feelings that leads to psychological problems. So, rather than considering uncomfortable and unpleasant feelings and experiences as abnormal, we should learn to accept them. Painful emotions and events are inevitable, and if they can be accepted rather than avoided, they can help personal growth.

Gestalt therapy

In the years following the Second World War, society in the Western world became increasingly individualistic, and this was reflected in the prevalence of humanistic and existentialist thinking in psychology. Among the new forms of "talking cure" to emerge at this time was Gestalt therapy, developed by Fritz Perls and his wife Laura.

What they proposed was a completely different approach to the traditional Freudian idea of unconscious drives, focusing instead on the way in which we view our experiences, our individual perception—hence the term "Gestalt," taken from Gestalt psychology (see page 110) with which it otherwise has little connection. Perls believed that we discover our own version of the "truth" of the world and our existence, living according to our own needs rather than seeking fulfillment through the values and ideas of others. It is up to each of us to take responsibility for controlling the way we perceive and react to the world, and learn to adjust to changing circumstances.

In Gestalt therapy's "empty chair" technique, patients address an empty chair to explore some aspect of their personality, thoughts, ideas, emotions, or a significant person.

"The Other"

Despite being an avid admirer of Freudian psychodynamic theory, French psychoanalyst Jacques Lacan upset many traditionalists with his ideas of the nature of the unconscious. In almost every version of psychoanalysis the unconscious is where our innermost thoughts and feelings reside, and it is an aspect of our self that communicates with the conscious self.

Lacan argued, however, that it was a mistake to think ourselves exist totally separately from the external world. We can only define ourselves as distinct from everything else—"the Other"—by recognizing its existence. We only have a sense of self if we have a concept of the Other. We acquire an understanding of the Other from the way it presents itself to us—signs that Lacan called its "discourse." Because our understanding of the Other defines ourselves, our inner world—the unconscious—is constructed in terms of the Other. We can only think and communicate in the language of the Other, and the unconscious can only express itself via this discourse.

a

A

"autre"
The "little Other"

"Autre"
"The Other"

Lacan frequently used algebraic notation for his concepts. Here the "little other" is a projection of the ego, while "the Other" exists in the realm of the symbolic.

The myth of
mental illness

Alongside the evolution of psychoanalysis, psychiatry in the 20th century became recognized as an increasingly important branch of medicine. The two fields often seem directly opposed, with psychiatrists dismissing psychodynamic theory as unscientific, and psychoanalysts rejecting the idea that psychological disorders are illnesses requiring medical treatment. Psychiatrist Thomas Szasz spearheaded the movement against classifying mental disorders as illness. His books *The Myth of Mental Illness* (1961) and *The Manufacture of Madness* (1970) argued that except for a few diseases that cause physical damage to the brain, there is no objectively verifiable way to diagnose mental illness. Though a patient may present the symptoms of an illness, these are better described as "problems in living" (Szasz rejected the term "mental disorder"). Just as religion has branded abnormal behavior as evidence of possession and science stigmatized disturbing behavior as insanity, psychiatry is now marginalizing sections of society by labeling them as mentally ill on scant evidence.

Throughout much of history sufferers of mental disorders have been stigmatized and often locked up or forced to endure dreadful conditions.

Antipsychiatry

Thomas Szasz' (see page 180) based his outright rejection of the notion of mental illnesses on the fact that there was no pathological evidence for their existence, but his views had a social and political dimension, too. By labeling certain behaviors as symptoms of illness requiring medical treatment, psychiatry could be used as a means of social control—which Szasz said was happening both under repressive regimes and in the so-called Free World.

Many psychologists (and even some psychiatrists) agreed, and in the 1960s an antipsychiatry movement gained momentum, led in Britain by psychiatrists such as R.D. Laing and David Cooper. Laing took Szasz's ideas further, saying that psychiatry diagnosed mental illness from behavioral symptoms and not physiologically, yet treated it biologically. He was opposed to the use of antipsychotic drugs and invasive surgery, arguing that psychiatry should examine the social and cultural factors which he claimed were the root causes of mental distress.

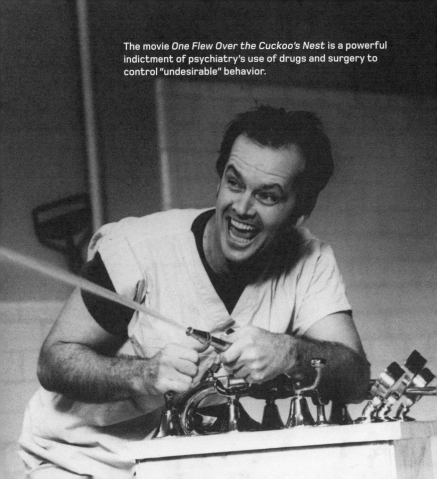

The movie *One Flew Over the Cuckoo's Nest* is a powerful indictment of psychiatry's use of drugs and surgery to control "undesirable" behavior.

Transactional analysis

While the emphasis in psychoanalysis in the latter part of the 20th century tended to be on the individual, Canadian-born psychiatrist Eric Berne focused his attention on relationships and interactions between individuals. He noted that these interactions, or "transactions," follow a limited number of patterns in everyday situations. In a hugely popular book *The Games People Play* (1964), Berne outlined how these patterns, which he labeled as "games," can be recognized by the technique of transactional analysis.

In any "game," each actor is at any time taking the role of one of three "ego-states": the Parent (either critical and authoritarian, or nurturing); the Adult (the voice of reason and reality); or the Child (either natural and uninhibited or willing to adapt to others). Each of these aspects of ourselves has its own way of dealing with situations. The pattern a transaction takes is determined by the ego-states the two participants adopt, for example Parent to Child, or Adult to Adult.

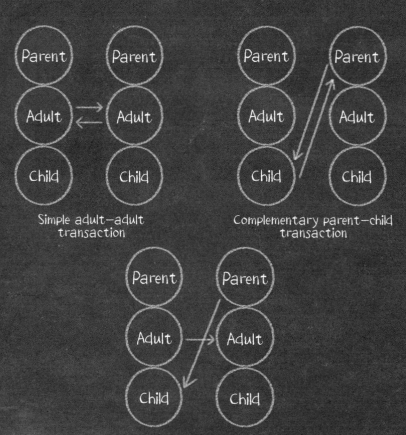

Simple adult–adult
transaction

Complementary parent–child
transaction

Crossed transaction

Social psychology

In the early years of psychology, psychologists studied the behavior and mental processes of individuals in isolation. It gradually became obvious, however, that interaction with other people affects these processes. In the 1930s, social psychology established itself as a distinct field of study. This examines the way that we think and behave in response to other people, in groups, or one-to-one, and how our thoughts, ideas, and attitudes influence the way we interact with others.

From early studies of how performance is affected by the presence of other people, through to Kurt Lewin's pioneering work on the behavior of small groups, social psychology has expanded to encompass subjects such as conformity and obedience, antisocial and prosocial behavior, attitudes and persuasion, and interpersonal relationships. The psychology of social interactions has influenced thinking in other branches of psychology. In the commercial world it has informed attitudes to management, organizational structures, and advertising.

The drama in *Twelve Angry Men* pivots on the interaction between individuals as a jury struggle to reach a consensus.

Performance

The earliest social psychology study was conducted in 1898 by Norman Triplett in the USA. He observed that cyclists achieved better speeds when riding with other cyclists than riding alone. In experiments with children turning a fishing reel, he found that it was not a matter of competitiveness—the mere presence of others increases performance.

Further research was done in the 1920s by Floyd Allport, one of the first true social psychologists, who found that performance in many different types of tasks was improved when done in groups—an effect he called "social facilitation." Although Triplett and Allport identified the phenomenon of social facilitation, theories for its cause did not arise until the 1960s. Robert Zajonc's "activation theory" arose from experiments with cockroaches that suggested that the presence of others acts as an arousal. However, while this arousal improves performance of simple or well-rehearsed tasks, it can impair performance of more complex or new ones.

Social loafing

One of the first studies of how being part of a group affects behavior was conducted not by a psychologist, but an agricultural engineer. In 1913, Max Ringelmann discovered that a group of men pulling on a rope exerted less effort collectively than when each pulled on his own. It was not clear, however, whether this "Ringelmann effect" was down to a lack of coordination between team members or poorer individual performance. More sophisticated replications of Ringelmann's experiment in the 1970s showed it to be "social loafing"— people in groups are less motivated to put in effort than when they act alone. Bibb Latané tested the effect in other tasks and found that blindfolded individuals wearing headphones shouted or clapped less loudly when they believed that they were doing so in a group, and their individual contribution was not identifiable. Latané concluded that the reduction in performance is not so much "freeloading," as a sharing of the pressure and responsibility to perform. Increasing the number of people in the group leads to less effort from each member.

Working in groups

The modern field of social psychology is generally considered to have been founded on the work of Kurt Lewin, a Jewish psychologist who emigrated to the USA in 1933. Lewin had a background in behaviorism (see page 46) and Gestalt psychology (see page 110), and was one of the first to study groups scientifically—how they are formed and maintained, and the nature of interactions within them and with other groups.

A group is a collection of individuals who come together with a common purpose or shared values and beliefs. This definition encompasses informal social groups, sporting teams, religious or political groups, and working groups. Lewin's particular interest was the underlying processes of interaction that shape a group and keep it together, how members become interdependent, and how the thoughts and actions of members are influenced by the group as a whole. He coined the term "group dynamics" to describe the way in which group members form a common perception and react to changing situations.

Field theory

Lewin was anxious to give a strict scientific basis for his theories, and believed that the influences on a group's behavior could be expressed in mathematical terms as "forces" analogous to those in physics and engineering. Different circumstances act as forces on both individuals and groups and can either be driving forces, assisting movement toward a goal, or restraining forces, hindering that movement.

These physical and social forces act upon the "field" of the group or individual, which as well as its goals and aspirations includes its hopes, fears, needs, motives, values, and beliefs (an idea adapted from Gestalt theories of perception). A person's field, which Lewin called a "life space," is constantly changing in reaction to external forces, shaping ideas, attitudes, and behavior depending on the degree to which the external circumstances are internalized. From this idea, Lewin developed a process of force-field analysis to assess the effects of external stimuli on individual and group behavior.

FORCE-FIELD
ANALYSIS

Driving forces

Equilibrium

Retraining
forces

Supporting
factors that
help drive change

Complicating
factors that
hinder change

Teams and leaders

From his detailed studies of groups and group dynamics, Lewin developed ideas that not only inspired a new field of psychological research, but also influenced the management of organizations. Of particular interest was "group cohesion," the processes—such as solidarity, morale, and team spirit—that make individuals want to stick together. For a group to function as a team, it is not enough for them to share a common goal or belief; the individual members need to feel a necessary part of the group, and realize that their own well-being is dependent on the well-being of the group as whole.

Australian psychologist Elton Mayo discovered that a hierarchy tends to evolve in any group, and a leadership structure emerges—formally or informally—to encourage group cohesion. A good leader recognizes the different needs of the group: task needs (what has to be done to achieve objectives); group needs, such as encouraging collaboration; and individual needs (what each member hopes to get from the task).

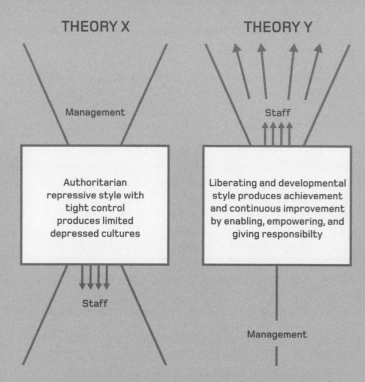

The two basic styles of management, according to Douglas McGregor, are Theory X (authoritarian) where a manager assumes his team is lazy, or Theory Y (collaborative) where team members are trusted.

A desire to conform

Lewin's pioneering work on social groups was directed mainly toward the influence of the individual members on group dynamics, and how a group reacted to changing circumstances, both collectively and individually. Other social psychologists, notably Muzafer Sherif and Solomon Asch, shifted attention from this to how the thoughts and behavior of an individual are affected by being a member of a social group. Asch noticed that, quite apart from the common interests that cause a group to come together, the members have a tendency to conform to the perceived norms of the group. This is different from compliance (voluntary assent) and obedience (following orders), which was later studied by Stanley Milgram (see page 208). In fact, the desire to conform is often strong enough to override personal values and perceptions, prompting individuals to do and even think things that go against their natural beliefs. While this tendency can be a positive force in maintaining group cohesion, Asch also acknowledged the dangers of the social influence of a need for conformity.

The power of conformity

Solomon Asch confirmed his ideas about conformity in a series of experiments conducted in the 1950s. Participants were told that they were taking part in a study of simple perception and were placed in groups without knowing that the group was made up of "stooges." The group was then tasked to compare the lengths of lines drawn on 18 cards, where it was obvious what the right answer was in each case.

The "real" participant was asked for his answer after most of the rest of the group, and after six trials the stooges began to give deliberately wrong answers. In more than a third of the trials, the participants gave an obviously incorrect answer in order to conform to the majority opinion, and three-quarters of the participants did so at least once. Interviewed afterward, some participants admitted they had realized their answer was wrong, but went along with the others because they hadn't wanted to seem different or foolish. Others, however, reported that they did not realize they had given incorrect answers.

Groupthink

Conformity has a useful social function in reinforcing group cohesion, which can help a group achieve its objectives but can also have a negative influence. Asch's conformity experiments—conducted during the McCarthy era in the USA —confirmed that individuals can convince themselves that they agree with what they perceive as the majority opinion. When this happens, there is a risk of what journalist William H. Whyte described as "groupthink"—faulty and irrational decision-making due to an exaggerated desire for cohesion. The social psychologist Irving Janis pointed out that pressure to conform amounts almost to obedience and independent rational thought is overridden. Decisions, even obviously bad ones, can be unanimously endorsed, and soon the group thinks it can do no wrong. Groupthink also promotes a tendency to exclude "black sheep" dissenters and be combative toward other groups. Janis suggests that these problems can be avoided by having an impartial leader who encourages debate, appoints a "devil's advocate," or consults with people outside the group.

Ingroups and outgroups

Another negative consequence of groupthink is the formation of "ingroups" and "outgroups." In a famous study of boys at summer camp in 1961, Muzafer Sherif showed that intergroup conflict is a result of competition for resources. The boys, aged 11 and 12, were divided into two groups on arrival at the camp. Neither group knew of the other's existence, and for the first phase of the experiment both groups pursued various activities quite separately. The groups developed team spirit and names—the Eagles and the Rattlers.

In the second phase, Sherif brought the two groups together for competitions with prizes for the winning group, and at this stage prejudices began to show, becoming increasingly aggressive. Even in a cooling-off period after the competition, the boys continued to rate their own group's abilities more highly than the other and referred to the other team in unfavorable terms. The conflict was not resolved until the two groups were forced to work together for a common goal.

Just following orders?

During the Nuremberg trials, many observers were shocked that apparently ordinary people had been capable of such inhuman cruelty. In their defense, many of the accused stated that they were simply following orders. For social psychologists, the question was: how much can our willingness to obey authority influence our behavior? It had already been established that a desire for conformity in social groups can override our personal values and beliefs, so it seemed likely that obedience could have a similar effect.

In a famous series of experiments, Stanley Milgram found that all the participants would administer painful electric shocks to an innocent person when told to do so (see page 208). The uncomfortable conclusion of this and similar experiments is that we have a tendency to obey what we perceive as authority figures. We learn obedience from an early age, in the family, at school, and society at large, and it is so ingrained in us that obeying can be a stronger force than our autonomy.

Electric shock experiments

Stanley Milgram's famous electric shock experiments set out to discover how far people would go in obeying an authority figure. Participants were assigned the role of "teacher," while a second participant (actually one of Milgram's confederates) received the role of "learner" in a rigged drawing of lots. The pair were put into adjoining rooms connected by an intercom. The learner was connected to electrodes, and the teacher shown a device that he or she was led to believe delivered electric shocks ranging from 15 volts (labeled: "Slight Shock"), 375 volts ("Danger: Severe Shock"), to 450 volts ("XXX"). Under instructions from an experimenter, the teacher set the learner a series of verbal tasks, and for each wrong answer was told to administer increasingly strong shocks; in response the learner feigned ever more distressed cries of pain. If the teacher was reluctant to continue, the experimenter issued a series of increasingly firm orders. Disturbingly, all the participants continued to 300 volts before refusing to continue and two-thirds went to the 450-volt limit.

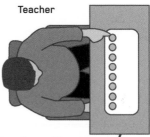

Teacher

Experimenter

Wall separating the learner from the experimenter and teacher

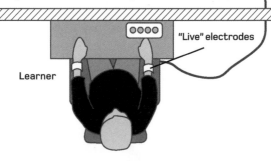

"Live" electrodes

Learner

Obedience and responsibility

The results of Milgram's electric shock experiments were a cause for serious concern. He had concluded that ordinary people show "a willingness to go to almost any lengths on the command of an authority," and that this demanded an urgent explanation. Obedience, he believed, is linked to responsibility, and people are more willing to obey when they can pass responsibility for their actions onto those giving the orders. In later versions of the shock experiments, many reluctant participants went onto administer apparently lethal shocks after the experimenter explicitly said that he would take responsibility for what happened, or refused to continue if he said the responsibility was the participant's own. Milgram explained that we behave in one of two ways in social situations: we act autonomously, taking responsibility for the consequences of our actions, or we act as "agents" for other people, shifting the responsibility to them. But before we act as another's agent, we need to recognize his or her authority as legitimate, morally or legally, and believe that he or she carries responsibility for any consequences.

The Stanford prison experiment

A decade after Milgram's obedience experiments, his high school classmate Philip Zimbardo devised the Stanford prison experiment to study another aspect of what makes good people do bad things. The 24 participants, students at Stanford University, were randomly divided into groups of "guards" and "prisoners," and put into a mock prison facility. Guards were issued with uniforms, sunglasses, whistles, handcuffs, and night-sticks. The prisoners—referred to by number rather than name—were stripped, searched, put into uniforms, and fitted with an ankle chain.

Given no specific instructions, both guards and prisoners adapted to their roles. The guards, without exception, became increasingly authoritarian and abusive, and the prisoners reacted to the sadistic punishment with rebellion, but also acute distress. Zimbardo had planned the experiment to take two weeks, but in only a few days several prisoners became so traumatized it was abandoned before the first week was up.

The power of social situation

The Stanford prison experiment became notorious for the disturbing behavior shown by the participants, and the psychological pain caused. But it demonstrated dramatically what happens when good people are put in an evil situation. While Asch and Milgram had shown that conformity and obedience can make people do things that contradict their values and beliefs, Zimbardo's study showed that there are situational pressures, too.

Ordinary people very quickly adopt the social role that is assigned to them. If they find themselves in a subordinate role, they will obey authority figures; however, when put in a social role of authority, they will not only use their power but also often abuse it. The power of social and institutional forces to influence behavior is especially noticeable when a social role removes a person's individuality (as the uniforms did). In a process of "de-individuation," personal identity is overwhelmed by the demands of the social role and situation.

Aggression and antisocial behavior

The studies by Asch, Milgram, and Zimbardo examined the social forces of conformity, obedience, and situation that can influence our actions, but did not provide a complete explanation for aggression and antisocial behavior. Some psychologists, such as Konrad Lorenz, explained aggression as an instinctive survival mechanism, while Albert Bandura (see page 268) believed that aggressive behavior is learned from others. John Dollard and Neal E. Miller looked for the social forces that prompt aggression, suggesting that aggression is the result of frustration. When our efforts and desires are blocked, we direct our aggression against whatever is preventing our satisfaction—and if it is our own fault we find a scapegoat. For Leonard Berkowitz, this was only a partial explanation. He believed that frustration leads to anger rather than aggression, and that anger is just one of a number of pains that provoke an aggressive reaction. To actually behave aggressively, there has to be an external cue, such as a weapon, loud noise, or bad smell that arouses aggressive thoughts.

Altruism and prosocial behavior

Following the Second World War, much social psychology focused, unsurprisingly, on understanding what social forces influenced ordinary people to behave in violent and antisocial ways. For the most part, however, people behave kindly to one another and our social institutions rely upon cooperation and prosocial behavior as much as the obligations of conformity and obedience.

For evolutionary psychologists, such altruistic behavior is "hardwired." Other social psychologists proposed a social exchange theory—the costs and rewards of our actions are carefully weighed, and that apparent altruism is never more than what is ultimately beneficial to ourselves. Not everyone agreed with this cynical interpretation of prosocial behavior. C. Daniel Batson believed that we are capable of truly altruistic behavior, stemming from our ability to empathize with others. Our empathetic concern for the needs or distress of other people acts as a motivating drive for acts of kindness and help.

The bystander effect

In New York in 1964, 37 people witnessed the murder of a young woman, but only one (reluctantly) later called the police. The incident prompted psychologists Bibb Latané and John Darley to examine why it is that people often do not offer assistance or want to get involved. They discovered the "bystander effect"—the more bystanders the lower the chances of help being offered. Similar to Latané's theories of social loafing (see page 190), it seems people feel less individually responsible the more others there are present.

Latané and Darley identified the cognitive and behavioral processes that precede bystander intervention. Firstly, the situation is noticed, then an emergency recognized, before the degree of responsibility is assessed, and a course of action decided on. Bystanders also make a judgment about the nature of the person requiring assistance—someone is more likely to get assistance if they are obviously elderly or disabled than if they are carrying a bottle of alcohol.

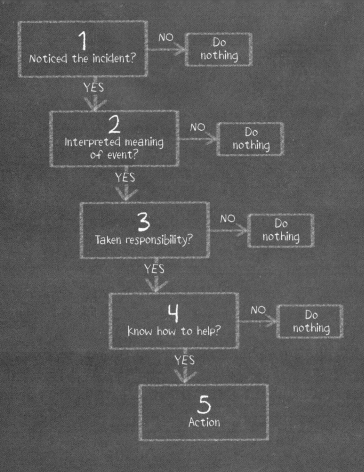

Attitudes

Social psychologists understand attitudes to be our positive and negative opinions of other people, issues, and objects, made up of a combination of our beliefs and values. They are built up over time, partly from rational appraisal, but are also learned from the values and beliefs of family and community. Attitudes form an important part of our concept of ourselves, and can become deeply ingrained and resistant to change, overriding rational thinking and leading to prejudiced views.

Naturally, attitudes influence our actions, but attitudes in general are an unreliable predictor of behavior. Just as our attitudes are shaped by conforming to social norms, we tend to behave in line with the norms of any situation, without changing our underlying attitude. In time, the values and beliefs of social groups—prejudice against ethnic minorities, for example—change, and the attitudes of individual members gradually change too. In some cases, individual attitudes can be changed by various methods of persuasion (see page 224).

Persuasion

In the 1930s, John B. Watson (see page 58) demonstrated that customers could be persuaded to buy products by appealing to basic emotions of love, fear, or anger, or by an endorsement by an authority. Other psychologists were interested in how the methods of persuasion could change attitudes and began a systematic study. Their interest was sparked by the widespread use of propaganda in Nazi Germany, the USSR, and communist China.

Certain elements of this propaganda were seen to be common to all techniques of persuasion, concerning not only the content of the message and the circumstances, but also who delivers it, its intended audience, and means of distribution. As Watson had shown, we are more likely to be persuaded by an emotional than a rational argument, such as fear of a scapegoated enemy, or the consequences of not voting a particular way—especially if it is delivered by an authoritative or charismatic source.

As well as using the techniques of persuasion to sell products, powerful propaganda uses authority figures to change people's attitudes.

Cognitive dissonance

The more deeply held an attitude, the less likely it is to be changed by persuasion, or changing social norms. Some beliefs are so strongly held that they are not shaken even by factual evidence that contradicts them, and may become more firmly entrenched when challenged. Leon Festinger, a student and later colleague of Kurt Lewin, described this as "cognitive dissonance"—the uncomfortable feeling we have when there is an inconsistency between our beliefs and facts.

To lessen the discomfort of cognitive dissonance, we can accept new evidence, and change our beliefs, or simply deny its truth. Alternatively, we can find ways of making the evidence consistent with the belief. Often our attitudes and beliefs are central to our identity, and so are stubbornly defended. A person with strong opinions is unlikely to listen to contradictory arguments, or will question their validity. When faced with incontrovertible facts, alternative explanations are sought, rather than giving up beliefs in which so much is invested.

Young Earth creationists must ignore or deny the facts of evolution in order to avoid uncomfortable truths and lessen the feeling of cognitive dissonance.

When prophecy fails

Festinger saw an opportunity to study cognitive dissonance when, in 1954, he came across a group prophesying the end of the world. The leader of the cult, Dorothy Martin, claimed she had received messages from aliens telling her that there would be an apocalyptic flood on December 21, wiping out all life except that of the true believers. These would be rescued by flying saucers. With colleagues, Festinger conducted a close study of the cult, before and after the predicted date of the destruction, written up in the book *When Prophecy Fails*.

Many of Martin's followers had sold up their possessions and left their jobs in preparation, but December 21 passed without incident. As Festinger's theory of cognitive dissonance predicted, rather than change minds, failure of the prediction prompted a reinterpretation of the facts. Martin insisted the Earth had been spared because of the activities of the cult—the members did not lose faith, but believed even more fervently and continued to preach their message.

The $1 or $20 experiment

Cognitive dissonance—the uncomfortable mental state of inconsistency between belief and evidence—not only occurs with deeply held beliefs, but can also influence our attitudes in many situations. Festinger devised experiments in which students were set an hour of very boring and repetitive tasks. At the end, some participants were asked to tell the next participant (actually a confederate of Festinger) that the task was interesting and enjoyable, creating dissonance between their recommendation and their experience.

Half of these were paid $1 to tell this lie, and half $20. As Festinger predicted, those paid $1 recommended the task in more favorable terms than those paid $20. The lower paid felt the dissonance more, and to reduce it changed their evaluation of the task to be consistent with their behavior in recommending it. The larger payment provided a justification for having done the tedious job, and so reduced the dissonance, meaning those paid $20 felt less need to recommend the task.

Interpersonal attraction

Much of social psychology is concerned with the interactions within and between social groups, but another area of interest is the way in which we form one-to-one relationships, especially our choice of sexual partners and spouses. Among the many aspects of interpersonal relationships is attraction —what draws people together in the first place. From an evolutionary perspective, interpersonal attraction is driven by the desire to choose a mate who will produce the fittest, healthiest offspring, and is primarily physical, sexual attraction.

Social psychologists have shown that there are also many social factors involved. Contrary to the popular notion that opposites attract, psychologists have found that attraction is more likely between people who come from similar social backgrounds, and have common attitudes, beliefs, and social standing. Attraction to another person may then develop into one of many different forms of loving relationship, described by Robert Sternberg as "Romantic," "Companionate," and "Fatuous."

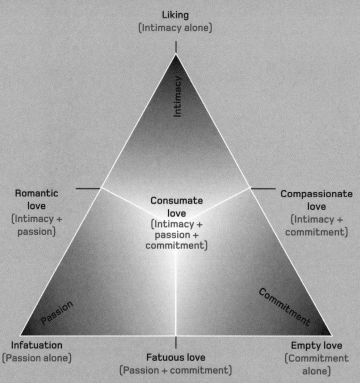

The different types of love are determined by the presence or absence of passion, intimacy, and commitment. Strong relationships are built on a combination of all three.

Long-term relationships

In many cultures, including Western society until comparatively recently, attraction and love are not considered a sufficient basis for a long-term relationship or marriage. Several societies have a tradition of "matchmaking" and arranged marriages, in which the social compatibility of the partners is more important than mutual attraction. The idea persists, even in modern liberal societies. According to social exchange theory, interpersonal relationships are based on a rational cost-benefit analysis. After a period of initial attraction, the parties can weigh up whether it is worth their while continuing with the relationship, which if it continues becomes based on common benefits rather than exchange. Other theories, less cynically, suggest that successful long-term relationships tend to follow a pattern. The beginning of a relationship is characterized by physical and sexual attraction—passion and intimacy over commitment. Over time, passion subsides, and social compatibility becomes more important. Commitment shifts the type of love from Romantic to Companionate.

Developmental psychology

Developmental psychology, like social psychology, did not emerge as a distinct branch of psychology until the 1930s. Before then, the process of growing up was treated as either a matter of learning, explained by the theories of behaviorism, or of psychosexual development as described by Freud. Jean Piaget's idea that our psychological makeup changes as we

grow up challenged conventional wisdom. It inspired the establishment of the new branch of developmental psychology, examining how these changes influence the way we learn. Since Piaget, the field of study has expanded to include the psychological changes at all stages throughout our lives, from the mother–baby bond to the potential problems of old age. Developmental psychologists have broadened the subject to cover all aspects of cognitive, emotional, and moral development, and how this is affected by our social and cultural environment—for example, acquisition of prejudices or differences in development between the sexes.

Nature vs. nurture

Arguments over whether knowledge is innate or acquired have raged since the time of Plato and Aristotle, but were given some scientific grounding in the 19th century by Darwin's theories of evolution. Francis Galton, a cousin of Darwin, coined the phrase "nature versus nurture" to describe the opposing scientific theses of environmental and inherited influences on development. He concluded that both play a part—certain innate characteristics are built on as we go through life.

In psychology, the debate became polarized into behaviorism (nurture), versus cognitive and evolutionary psychology (nature). Developmental psychology, however, has tended to examine the relationship between genetically inherited and environmental influences. One of the ways that psychologists can investigate this is in studies of twins (a method pioneered by Galton). Twins brought up together can have matched environmental influences, while identical twins separated at an early age offer a window into the effects of different environments.

Attachment and separation

The influences of both nature and nurture on psychological development can be seen in children at a very early age. The bond between an infant and its caregiver, usually its mother, is a strong impulse for the protection and survival of the child. This attachment, as John Bowlby called it, is inborn and genetically programed, and the nature of the attachment affects aspects of further development.

Bowlby developed his ideas in the UK after the Second World War, observing the effects on children who were separated from their parents through evacuation and being orphaned. Fundamental to his theory was the idea that a mother, or primary caregiver, provides the child with a sense of physical, emotional, and psychological security. This gives the infant a secure base to return to as it explores its environment. If this attachment is disrupted, inconsistent, or irregular, or in extreme cases completely absent, it can affect the child's subsequent development and ability to form relationships.

Different kinds of attachment

Bowlby's study of "maternal deprivation" and the attachment theory he developed from it was taken up by his colleague Mary Ainsworth. They had noticed that although attachment provides a secure physical and emotional base, it is normal for a child to experience anxiety when separated from its mother. Ainsworth discovered that even in apparently normal mother–child relationships, attachment varies according to the degree the mother responds to her child's emotional and psychological needs. She identified three basic styles of attachment: secure, anxious–avoidant, and anxious–resistant (to which a colleague added a fourth: disorganized attachment). In a secure attachment, the most healthy form, the mother is sensitive to the needs of the child, who then trusts the parent as a secure base. With inadequate or inconsistent care, the child develops insecure anxious–avoidant attachment, and may become indifferent to its mother to avoid the anxiety of separation. The attachment may become anxious–resistant, so that the child clings to its mother, and is distressed by separation.

The Strange Situation experiment

The different types of attachment were first identified in a series of experiments conducted by Ainsworth in the 1960s and 70s. She used a procedure that became known as the "Strange Situation" to examine the anxiety and stress levels of infants left to explore alone, with a stranger and when reunited with their mothers. In each experiment, a mother and child were put into a room with toys, and the infant left to explore in his mother's presence. A stranger then entered the room, and interacted first with the mother, then the child. The mother left the child with the stranger, but returned later to reassure or comfort the child. The child was then left alone to play, joined again by a stranger, and finally the mother returned. Ainsworth noted the amount the child explored independently at each stage, and particularly its distress levels at being separated from its mother—both when left with the stranger and when left alone—and its reaction on being reunited with her. The children's behavior fits into three patterns, which Ainsworth identified as the three basic attachment types.

Ainsworth's Strange Situation Assessment

1. Parent and infant are alone in a room

2. Stranger joins parent and infant

3. Parent leaves infant and stranger alone

4. Parent returns and stranger leaves room

5. Parent leaves and infant left alone in room

6. Stranger returns

7. Parent returns and comforts child

Cupboard love?

At the time Bowlby was developing his attachment theory, John B. Watson's extreme ideas of behaviorist childcare (see page 64) held sway. The notion of attachment was accepted, but as an instinctive mechanism with evolutionary purpose, and centered on feeding and physical protection of the child. Influenced by Bowlby's ideas, Harry Harlow set out to show the importance of comfort and security in attachment.

In a series of experiments Harlow provided infant macaque monkeys with surrogate mothers, either made from bare wood and wire, or covered in soft material. In some experiments, the wire "mother" held a feeding bottle and the cuddly mother did not, but although the baby monkeys fed from the bottles, they preferred to spend time clinging to the comforting soft "mother." Harlow discovered that the infants formed an attachment with the cuddly surrogate mothers, but this was not the case with the "mothers" that simply provided nourishment. Harlow's experiments confirmed Bowlby's theory.

Love and comfort are essential components of mother–child attachment. This realization influenced a change in attitudes to childcare.

Parent or caregiver

Almost all the early research into attachment and infant development focused on the mother–child relationship. Psychologists acknowledged that attachment occurred between a child and its primary caregiver, which might be the father, another family member, or an adoptive parent, but generally assumed a "normal" situation of mother and child. The implication was that any separation distress and psychological disorders were specifically caused by maternal deprivation.

This was disputed by Michael Rutter and Bruno Bettelheim. Rutter's studies of children with mental health problems led him to the conclusion that it is the quality of care, rather than the identity of the caregiver, that is most influential on healthy development. This was confirmed by Bettelheim's studies of children brought up communally in kibbutzim. Where Rutter saw psychological damage in children brought up in institutions, Bettelheim found a caring environment produced children who formed close peer relationships and found success in adulthood.

Psychological stages

The turning point for developmental psychology came with Jean Piaget, a Swiss psychologist who suggested that just as there are fundamental physical differences between children and adults, so too are there psychological differences. Our mental development, he suggested, is not simply a question of learning, but our minds go through a process of change from infancy to adulthood.

Piaget's observations of children growing up and learning showed that the prevailing view of children as "miniature adults" was mistaken, and led him to conclude that their psychological development progressed in recognizable stages. At each stage, the child's mind works in a different way to absorb information from the external world, building cognitive, social, and motor skills. Contradicting the dominant behaviorist thinking of the time, Piaget observed that this progress was universal through all of the stages, suggesting that they are innate and genetically determined, not learned.

Stages of cognitive development

Piaget discovered that children develop their cognitive abilities in four distinct stages. Every child goes through the stages in the same sequence. Even though they only progress once a stage is successfully completed, in most children the changes seem to occur at about the same ages. During the first stage, infants learn about the external world through their senses and physical actions, and progress from simply discovering things to an intentional exploration and understanding of objects. Covering roughly the first two years of life, Piaget called this the sensorimotor stage. In the preoperational stage, they begin to use language and arrange objects in a rational way—according to color or size, for example. By about age seven, children enter the concrete operational stage, in which they gain an understanding of comparative quantities of objects and use logical reasoning. The formal operational stage starts around age 11, when children build on their ability to think logically, using verbal reasoning and imagination to think about abstract concepts.

The adolescent can reason abstractly and think in hypothetical terms.

Formal operational (11 years – adult)

The child can think logically about concrete objects and can thus add and subtract. The child also understands conversation.

Concrete operational (7–11 years)

The child uses symbols (words and images) to represent objects, but does not reason logically. The child also has the ability to pretend. During this stage, the child is egocentric.

Preoperational (2–7 years)

The infant explores the world through direct sensory and motor contact. Object permanence and separation anxiety develop during this stage.

Sensorimotor (birth – 2 years)

Development of concept of self

An important aspect noted by Piaget in each stage of a child's cognitive development is growing awareness of the world outside itself, and in particular a concept of itself and its place in the world. At birth, a child is totally egocentric, and in the first stage of development gradually learns to control its actions to explore objects, slowly becoming self-aware.

The child is still egocentric, however, even as it progresses into the preoperational stage, and is unable to see things from another person's perspective. It is not until a child enters the third stage and begins to use logical reasoning that it begins to understand relationships between objects, and slowly becomes aware of its own (relative) place in the world. When a child reaches the final stage and is capable of thinking hypothetically, it truly starts to overcome its egocentricity. Having in the previous three stages developed a concept of self, the child can now imagine itself in other people's shoes and appreciate more fully their perspective.

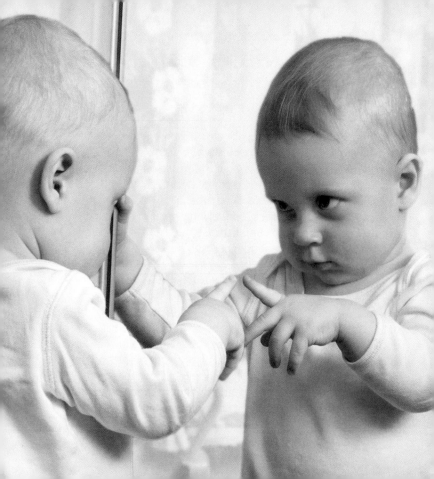

The child as scientist

Piaget's theory that cognitive development progresses in distinct stages has implications for the way that children should be taught. At each stage, there are certain abilities and skills that a child needs to master before it can progress to the next stage. The learning process moves in steps, each building on the one before. Education, therefore, must take account of these steps and be designed to assist the child to complete each step in sequence.

Piaget's ideas revolutionized education. He believed that learning is an exploratory process and not something that can be taught. The role of the educator—teacher or parent—is not to instruct, but to provide the child with an environment appropriate to its stage of development. This allows it to discover things as a scientist does, by experiment and hands-on experience. Child-centered schooling is centered on a child's changing intellectual needs and abilities, rather than assuming cognitive processes that are the same as an adult's.

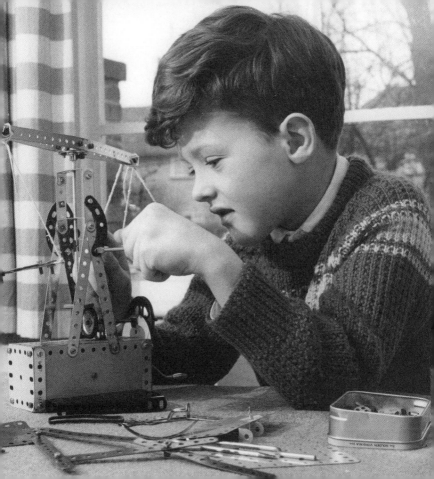

The child as apprentice

Following Piaget, it is now generally accepted that the cognitive processes of children are different from those of adults, and that there is a process of intellectual development. Many psychologists and educationalists have also adopted the model of development progressing in identifiable stages. However, not all agree with the notion that this is achieved by the individual discovering things through experience alone.

Lev Vygotsky, a psychologist working in Soviet Russia, saw this development as occurring on different levels. He believed that hands-on activities need not be solitary, and we learn and develop from doing things with our peers. He also said that instruction and supervision from an adult play an important part in nurturing a child's development. In place of Piaget's child-as-scientist metaphor, Vygotsky suggested that the child is an apprentice, learning from experience under the guidance of a "master." This was most necessary, he said, when a child is moving from a task it has mastered to learning a new one.

Cultural and historical development

After the so-called "cognitive revolution" in the 1950s, the idea of learning as a cognitive process began to influence developmental psychology. Jerome Bruner built on the pioneering work of Piaget and Vygotsky. He agreed with Vygotsky that a child develops both in isolation and socially, and suggested that guidance from elders gives development a historical and cultural context. Bruner, however, disagreed that there are distinct stages of intellectual development.

Instead of a linear progression of cognitive development, he believed that children gradually build on knowledge they have acquired, working from basic principles to more detailed and sophisticated knowledge and skills. This "scaffolding" process does not follow a rigid sequence, so children can learn things at any age, so long as the information presented to them is organized to follow from what has already been learned. Using this idea, Bruner devised a "spiral curriculum," which returns to first principles in each subject before introducing new material.

The "school of Vygotsky" holds that children acquire the thought
processes and behaviors of their society, meaning that learning varies
radically between cultures.

Stages of psychosocial development

Cognitive psychology was only one of the influences on ideas of development in the second half of the 20th century. Erik Erikson's theory of psychosocial development was modeled more on Freud's stages of psychosexual development (see page 150) than on Piaget, with each stage characterized by a "crisis" of two conflicting inner forces. Erikson suggested that it is not necessary to successfully complete a stage before moving onto the next (although failure may cause problems later), and that development continues into adult life. He identified eight stages, each posing the challenge of resolving its positive and negative attributes. In the first years of life, the infant develops a sense of trust, and goes on to tackle feelings of shame, doubt, and guilt to establish independence as an individual. At school, the child develops personal abilities, but at the same time begins to compare itself with others. As an adolescent, he or she tackles existential questions, before embarking on the adult challenges of forming relationships, having a family, and career. Finally, in old age, life is assessed retrospectively.

Stages of psychosocial development

Integrity vs. despair
Old age

Generativity vs. stagnation
Middle age

Intimacy vs. isolation
Young adult

Identity vs. role confusion
Adolescence

Industry vs. inferiority
School years

Initiative vs. guilt
Later childhood

Autonomy vs. shame and doubt
Early childhood

Trust vs. distrust
Infancy

Increases in complexity

Moral development

Piaget explained that as a child acquires abilities of logical reasoning and becomes less egocentric, it develops a sense of morality. Lawrence Kohlberg suggested that moral development evolves during three periods of our lives— childhood, adolescence, and adulthood. Each of these is marked by a particular level of moral reasoning ("preconventional," "conventional," and "postconventional"), divided into two stages. In childhood, moral reasoning is based on fixed rules and consequences. In the first stage this is determined by notions of obedience and punishment, while in the second stage morality is judged by the rewards it brings. The conventional level of moral reasoning incorporates an understanding of people's intentions. In the first, "good boy–nice girl" stage, the adolescent conforms to social norms, but this is replaced in the following stage by a respect for authority. A minority progress to the postconventional, or "principled" level, questioning conventional authority in the first stage, and finally allowing their own conscience determine their ethical principles.

Principle

Social contract

Law and order morality

"Good boy/nice girl" attitude

Self-interest

Avoiding punishment

Social learning theory

Although the theories of developmental psychologists greatly influenced educational thinking, in the area of moral development, behaviorist ideas of conditioning persisted. The conventional wisdom was that a sense of moral right and wrong was learned through rewards and punishments (reinforcement of operant conditioning) for good or bad behavior. Albert Bandura, however, felt that this was an oversimplification, and that almost all our behavior is learned socially by observing the behavior of other people.

Children are aware of what people around them, especially adults, are doing and saying. They remember it, rehearse it in their minds, modeling their actions on parents or other significant adult "role models." This process, according to Bandura's social learning theory, has four elements: attention (the child notices behavior); retention (child keeps it in mind); reproduction (child imitates it), and motivation (the behavior is seen to meet with approval or reward).

The Bobo doll experiment

Social learning theory emerged in the 1960s from the studies of Albert Bandura. The best known is his "Bobo doll" experiment, which examined aggressive behavior in children. The idea was simple. Boys and girls between the ages of three and six were each taken to a room equipped with toys and games. The control group were left to play, while others were accompanied by an adult who played in the "adult corner" with an inflated Bobo doll. In half of these cases, the adult became frustrated and aggressive, shouting at the Bobo doll, punching and kicking it, and hitting it with a mallet. In the other trials the adult behaved passively. Each child was then taken to another room to play, but interrupted (to induce frustration) and taken back to the first room. The children who had witnessed an adult model of aggressive behavior tended to take out their frustration on the Bobo doll, imitating the verbal and physical aggression and even inventing some aggressive acts of their own. Those who had not seen an adult behave aggressively only rarely showed any form of aggressive behavior.

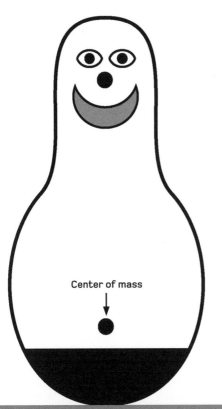

A low center of mass causes the Bobo doll to bob back into an upright position when it is struck.

Center of mass

Learning from the media

Bandura's social learning theory and the Bobo doll experiment had an especial relevance for its time and sparked a debate that continues to the present. TV and other forms of mass media were becoming all-pervasive. The extent to which children were being exposed to violent images was unprecedented (a concern mirrored more recently by the rise of disturbingly graphic video games). The idea that children model behavior on what they see suggests that this would lead to an increased tendency to aggressive behavior, but a number of studies have shown that this is not the case.

Some psychologists argue that violent images and games act as a "safety valve" for feelings of frustration and anger, leading to a decrease in aggressive behavior. Social learning theory advocates point out that children not only notice, but also evaluate the behavior around them, and have a good sense of its real-world relevance. Real-life violence is more likely to affect their behavior than violence portrayed in the media.

Gender development

Study of gender development, and ideas of sexual and gender identity, were largely overlooked by psychologists until the rise of second-wave feminism in the latter half of the 20th century. As well as physical differences between the sexes, we almost invariably make a distinction between the psychological makeup of males and females. Some people believe that our brains are "hardwired" for specific gender roles—female empathy contrasted with male systemizing, for example—perhaps with an evolutionary purpose.

Social learning theory, however, explains the psychological differences of gender identity (as opposed to physical sexual identity) as learned behavior. Children learn from adults the attributes and behavior—or sexual stereotypes—that are considered appropriate to their gender. Modeling themselves on adults of their own sex, they develop a concept of distinctly "masculine" or "feminine" traits. This process is reinforced by a tendency of adults to treat children along stereotypical lines.

The Baby X experiments

The influence of sexual stereotypes on gender development is somewhat circular. Children learn from adults the stereotypical attributes associated with their biological sexual identity and tend to imitate a same-sex role model. However, some of these attributes are to an extent imposed upon them too—adults treat male and female children differently.

In the 1970s, variations of the "Baby X" experiment showed that adults played differently with the same baby depending on whether they were told its sex or not. There was also a marked difference between the attitudes of the male and female adults to the child. As well as offering it stereotypically "gendered" toys—dolls or trucks, for example—there was a difference in the amount they talked to the child and made physical contact. From birth, children begin to develop a gender identity as adult expectations perpetuate sexual stereotypes, such as the submissive, emotional, and empathetic nature of girls and the independence, rationality, and toughness of boys.

Adolescence

One of the earliest pioneers of developmental psychology was G. Stanley Hall, the first person to be awarded a PhD in psychology in the USA. He was strongly influenced by Darwin's theory of evolution and believed that psychological development is a sort of evolution in miniature. He is especially known for his study of adolescence, which Hall described as a period of "Sturm und Drang" (storm and stress).

Adolescents, he said, go through a process of emotional upheaval caused by an increased awareness of self and environment, and their self-consciousness leads to sensitivity, depression, and recklessness. Hall's analysis of the stormy nature of adolescence has broadly been confirmed by later psychologists. Erik Erikson described the teenage years as a period characterized by the "crisis" of ego identity and role confusion, when the adolescent struggles with self-criticism and finding a place in the world. Erikson coined the term "identity crisis" specifically for this time of life.

Taking responsibility

For many psychologists, the idea of development meant the transition from birth through childhood and adolescence to maturity as an adult. Developmental psychology was mainly concerned with cognitive and intellectual development, which was considered complete once adulthood is reached. But since Erik Erikson proposed the idea (see page 262), it has become more accepted that we continue to develop all through our lives, experientially if not cognitively. After the stormy period of adolescence, we emerge as adults, but with a new set of conflicting challenges that necessitate a further period of psychological growth and development in young adulthood. This focuses primarily on forming and sustaining long-term relationships with friends, colleagues, and a life-partner, creating mutual trust and interdependence that gives a firm base from which to take on the responsibilities of family and career. If the lessons of adolescence have not been learned, lack of confidence and fear of commitment can lead to an inability to achieve the intimacy necessary for satisfactory relationships.

Middle age

We continue to face challenges that affect our psychological and emotional makeup throughout our adult lives. Although change and development are slower and maybe less noticeable than in the first couple of decades of life, they are no less profound. The period of middle adulthood can stretch from as early as age 25 to around 70, and comes as we establish long-term relationships, set up home and family, and settle into a career. According to Erikson, this stage is characterized by conflict between feelings of generativity or stagnation—the archetypal "mid-life crisis," when we realize we are no longer young. We can feel satisfaction from a sense of nurturing the next generation, and by being a useful and productive member of the community. By the same token, we can feel a sense of aimlessness and disappointment, especially if our careers plateau or from "empty nest syndrome" when children leave home. An inability to reconcile these conflicts can result in depression, or a need to recapture lost youth, which can prompt sudden changes and divorce, for example.

Old age

Even in old age, we face new psychological challenges that can be viewed as affecting our lifelong psychological development. This period of life is often associated with negative stereotypes of physical and intellectual deterioration, but just like any other stage of development it presents both positive and negative possibilities.

After retirement from a working life and bringing up a family, this can be a time for taking up new interests and doing things that we have not been able to before, or at last having the time for a more active social life. On the negative side, however, it is also when our bodies begin to slow down and become frailer, and when we may become isolated by the death or incapacity of our friends and partners. For most people, it is also a time for reflection, "putting one's house in order," and assessing how well our lives have been spent. This raises the possibility of a sense of integrity if we perceive our lives to have been successful, or despair if we feel we have not achieved our aims.

The "Ages of me"

In theories of developmental psychology, especially those describing distinct stages of development, it is impossible to pin down the exact ages at which changes occur—we are all different and develop at different rates. This raises the question of what is meant by "age." We have a chronological age, but we also have several different ages corresponding to our physical or psychological development.

In a study of aging and attitudes to age, Robert Kastenbaum examined these various "ages." In addition to chronological age, he asked about subjective age—the age that we feel—which he found tends to be younger than our actual age, especially as we get older. He also identified biological age, assessed by the state of our bodies and faces, either by ourselves or other people, our functional age, determined by our interests and activities, and our social life, which we judge by our position in society. The study found that these ages had a broad range, demonstrating the truism that we are only as old as we feel.

Psychology of difference

To a large extent, psychology is the science of how humans as a species think and behave. Humans are, however, all individuals, and each of us has a unique psychological makeup as distinct as our physical appearance. This is the province of what is often known as the "psychology of difference," which examines the things that distinguish us from one another, rather than the mental and behavioral characteristics we all have in common.

It is a broad field of study, identifying the psychological factors that vary from one person to another, such as intelligence and personality. Often these are difficult to define, and there is debate over whether they are innate or learned characteristics, and whether they are fixed or change with time. The psychology of difference also raises the question of what is considered normal or abnormal, whether our ideas of normality differ from one culture to another, and when individual "quirks" should be treated as disorders or illnesses.

The Marx Brothers play on the inherently comedic aspects of differences between people, constantly pricking notions of "normality."

Intelligence

Intelligence is something that we all think we can recognize, but is notoriously difficult to measure and even harder to define. In the late 19th century several psychologists attempted to find an objective measure of intelligence, using a variety of tests of cognitive abilities, leading to Wilhelm Wundt's proposal of an Intelligence Quotient (IQ) as a means of comparing intelligence between people. However, these tests, and most intelligence testing since, have failed to define exactly what they are measuring, leading Edwin Boring to his tongue-in-cheek definition of intelligence as "what intelligence tests measure." From the beginning of research into the subject, there has been lively debate around whether intelligence is innate and inherited. Alfred Binet, a French psychologist who devised intelligence tests that are still in use today, disagreed with the prevailing view that intelligence is fixed at birth. He suggested that our cognitive abilities change throughout life, and intelligence testing only measures those abilities at a specific time, and in a specific context.

Distribution of IQ scores

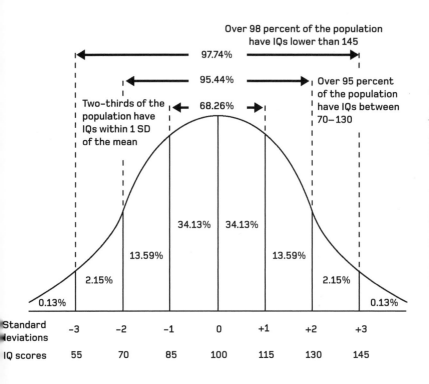

General vs. specific intelligence

Intelligence tests typically include a wide variety of mental tasks, testing verbal, mathematical, and spatial skills involving several different cognitive processes, including memory and knowledge as well as perception and reasoning. British psychologist Charles Spearman found that there was a positive correlation between abilities in these various different tasks, and suggested that there was a single common factor, a "general intelligence factor," which he labeled g.

General intelligence, he explained, can be measured by testing specific skills, which he labeled s, to distinguish them from g. Spearman believed that general intelligence is innate and determines performance in tests that involve a variety of learned mental abilities. People who display ability in a particular field may also score highly on tests of other specific abilities. Although later disputed, Spearman's idea of a general intelligence factor, like Wundt's idea of IQ, continues to be a model for popular ideas and definitions of intelligence.

Is there more than one kind of intelligence?

Spearman's "general intelligence factor" (g) influenced a particularly British view of intelligence as a single measurable quantity that is fixed and innate, and can be seen in an ability to perform a variety of cognitive tasks. This idea was expanded upon by Cyril Burt and Philip E. Vernon, who identified a number of factors that fall somewhere between g and s. Later L.L. Thurstone developed a model of seven separate areas of ability—verbal comprehension, verbal fluency, mathematical reasoning, inductive reasoning, spatial awareness, associative memory, memory, and perceptual speed —where g was the average of these abilities. The American psychologist J.P. Guilford rejected the idea altogether, instead suggesting that there are three different aspects of any cognitive task: content (what needs to be done); operations (how it can be done); and product (the results). According to Guilford, there are five different kinds of content, five kinds of operation and six kinds of product. In various combinations these give a total of 150 distinct cognitive abilities.

The idea that there are different kinds of intelligence stems from the fact that there is a wide range of cognitive talents at which different people excel.

Reinforcing cultural and racial prejudices

Research into intelligence, perhaps more than any other field of psychology, has attracted accusations of cultural and racial bias. The idea that intelligence is fixed and inherited fueled eugenics movements in the late 19th and early 20th centuries, while testing that appears to show the superior intelligence of white, Western, middle-class males has reinforced many cultural and racial prejudices.

When cognitive abilities singled out for testing are based on modern Western ideas of intelligence, people from other cultures are likely to score low, leading to results that imply that there are differences in intelligence between races, classes, and the sexes. However, most modern urban dwellers would score badly in tests of survival skills, reading a landscape, or plant and animal recognition, for example. Recently, psychologists have come to realize that intelligence is not as fixed as had been thought, and culture is a factor that has to be taken into account when attempting to measure it.

Dolly Parton is an example of an intelligent person who plays with preconceptions of intelligence. She says, "I'm not offended by all the dumb blonde jokes because I know I'm not dumb. And I also know I'm not blonde!"

Fluid or crystallized?

A British-born psychologist, Raymond Cattell, who spent most of his career in the USA, bridged the divide between Spearman's notion of general intelligence and Guilford's multifactor model. He suggested that there are broadly two different types of cognitive ability, which he called fluid intelligence (Gf) and crystallized intelligence (Gc). Fluid intelligence, he said, is the ability to solve new cognitive problems with reasoning, rather than knowledge or skills that have been learned. It is therefore true general intelligence free from any cultural bias and not influenced by education. On the other hand, crystallized intelligence is based on abilities learned throughout life—the knowledge and skills that have been taught or learned through experience. Cattell's model was expanded by John L. Horn and later refined by John B. Carroll in what became known as the Cattell-Horn-Carroll theory, which proposes a hierarchical list of cognitive abilities, ranging from g at the top through 10 broad categories of abilities as suggested by Horn (including Cattell's Gf and Gc).

Multiple intelligences

J.P. Guilford's suspicion of "general intelligence" (see page 292) resurfaced in the 1980s with Howard Gardner's theory of multiple intelligences. Unlike previous theories, Gardner said that we have various ways of tackling cognitive tasks, but ability in one is not related to ability in any of the others. Each of us has a different level of ability in each category of intelligence, contributing to our own unique combination of intelligences. He has so far identified eight independent intelligences: verbal/linguistic; logic/mathematical; musical; visual/spatial; bodily/kinesthetic; interpersonal or social; intrapersonal or self-reflective; and naturalistic. More recently, Gardner has suggested the list might be expanded to include existential/spiritual, moral, and pedagogical intelligence. Robert Sternberg similarly rejects the notion of a single, general intelligence. Instead, he proposes three basic categories: analytic intelligence (the ability to solve definite problems), synthetic intelligence (the ability to find creative solutions), and practical intelligence (the ability to apply knowledge and skills).

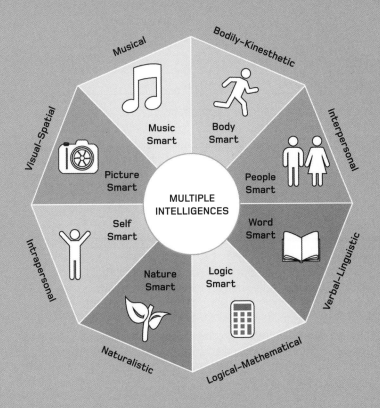

Is intelligence fixed, or can it be altered?

Theories of a general intelligence often assume that intelligence is more a product of nature than nurture, and consequently that it is a fixed characteristic. But just as the idea of general intelligence itself was disputed, so too was the emphasis on its genetic, inherited basis. Several studies showed that environment is at least as influential, and intervention can improve performance in IQ tests.

The Milwaukee project in 1968 involved 40 families from a deprived area of the inner city. The mothers of very young children were given a broad range of help to improve their social and financial situation, including job training and education. By the time their children reached school age, they had an above average IQ according to standard tests, and scored considerably higher than the children of a control group. Significantly, however, after starting at school, and the end of the project, the children's IQ levels gradually dropped to the below-average levels typical of the inner-city area.

Personality

Personality, perhaps more than intelligence, is what we feel is the essence of what makes each of us uniquely individual. However, like intelligence, it is an elusive concept—difficult to define and even more difficult to measure scientifically. Classical Greek philosophers explained personality in terms of four temperaments, an idea that has echoes in some modern psychological theories of personality.

Psychodynamic theories of personality evolved from Freud's explanation of conflict between our conscious and unconscious minds, emerging as mainstream theories in the second half of the 20th century. It is generally agreed today that personality is distinct from moods and emotions, but different theories and explanations of personality disagree on whether it is a fixed characteristic, or changes over time or even according to circumstances. Differences of opinion also arise over what degree of personality is innate, genetic, and inherited, and how much is shaped by our individual environments and experience.

1 Sanguin

2 Phlegmatique

3 Cholerique

4 Mélancolique

Traits

The groundbreaking work of brothers Gordon and Floyd Allport in the 1960s opened up the field of research into the psychology of personality. Gordon Allport thought that we recognize the elements that make up someone's personality, and reflect these in the way we describe them verbally. He scoured dictionaries, collecting several thousand descriptive words, which he said represented the "traits" that form our personalities. Some, he explained, are common to everyone, although to different degrees, while others are individual.

There are "cardinal traits," or "ruling passions," that may dominate other characteristics, and secondary traits that only manifest themselves when triggered by particular circumstances or situations. Somewhere between cardinal and secondary traits is the mixture of common traits that mostly define our personality. Allport's theory implied a range of different personalities, stemming from innumerable combinations of traits, rather than a set of fixed personality types.

Nervousness

Optimism

Impulsiveness

Empathy

Honesty

Timidity

Selfishness

Adaptabilty   Tolerance

Extraversion and neuroticism

In contrast to Allport's trait theory (see page 304), Hans Eysenck argued that there are just two factors that define personality type: extraversion (E) and neuroticism (N). These, in his opinion, are largely genetically determined and fixed characteristics. Extraverts are sociable, carefree, and fun-loving, and neurotics—in Eysenck's use of the term—are unstable, moody, and easily affected by their emotions.

Each of these dimensions of personality is a continuum, ranging from extravert to introvert, and neurotic to stable, which can be represented on a two-dimensional diagram. Each individual personality can be plotted, depending on the level of extraversion/introversion and stability/instability. The similarities with the ancient notion of four temperaments are striking, which Eysenck acknowledged. Although Eysenck's theory is sometimes described as a "type theory," he disliked the idea of personality types, preferring to see different personalities as points on a spectrum.

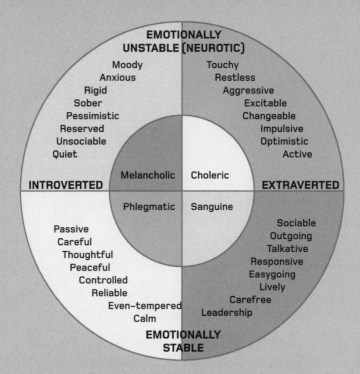

Someone who is both highly extravert and highly neurotic corresponds to a "choleric temperament"; an introverted, stable person is thought to have a "phlegmatic temperament" and so on.

The Big Five

Eysenck's analysis of personality was initially based on two factors, extraversion and neuroticism, but later he added a third dimension to his model, psychoticism (P). Those who score highly on a scale of P tend to be solitary, insensitive, hostile, and manipulative, so that the range of psychoticism includes psychiatric and behavior disorders at its higher levels.

Other psychologists since Eysenck have suggested that there are other "traits" that constitute basic parameters for assessing personality. The most widely used model today is based on the "Big Five," known by the acronym OCEAN: openness to experience, conscientiousness, extraversion, agreeableness, and neuroticism. Eysenck's E and N, are retained in this model, but in place of his "psychoticism" are conscientiousness and agreeableness (emphasizing the positive rather than negative end of the scale). In addition there is also "openness to experience," covering such traits as creativity, curiosity, and appreciation of intellectual pursuits.

Big Five

		Low scorers	High scorers
1	Openness to experience	Down-to-earth Uncreative Conventional Uncurious	Imaginative Creative Original Curious
2	Conscientiousness	Negligent Lazy Disorganized Late	Conscientious Hardworking Well-organized Punctual
3	Extraversion	Loner Quiet Passive Reserved	Joiner Talkative Active Affectionate
4	Agreeableness	Suspicious Critical Ruthless Irritable	Trusting Lenient Soft-hearted Good-natured
5	Neuroticism	Calm Even-tempered Comfortable Unemotional	Worried Temperamental Self-conscious Emotional

Personal construct theory

Many psychologists attempted to find an objective way of defining and assessing personality, by seeing it as something that is perceived by other people. George A. Kelly on the other hand felt that we perceive our own personality from the inside, subjectively, and this shapes the way that we view the world. In his personal construct theory, personality is not inherited or even environmentally shaped, but results from cognitive processes. We experience and explore the world and each make a personal interpretation of what we discover.

Our interpretations color our subsequent perception and behavior, so that we see the world through our own personally constructed "goggles." The better the world fits our expectations, the more it confirms our beliefs and attitudes, and influences the behavior that others perceive as our personality. Personal construct theory is therefore a comprehensive system of psychology that can be used to identify the constructs an individual uses to interpret the world and other people.

Personality and situation

Most theories of personality, whether of numerous traits, or of a limited number of types, imply that it is permanent and stable, and that we behave in a consistent way according to these fixed characteristics. But even Allport in his trait theory recognized that personality is not invariable—his "secondary traits" only show themselves in certain situations.

Later, several psychologists took the view that personality is revealed by behavior according to situation. Walter Mischel took this "situationist" stance even further, suggesting that rather than personality traits being something that a person possesses, they are what the person does: cognitive processes associated with a situation. A person's behavior, by which we judge their personality, is determined by their cognitive appraisal of a situation and not an innate tendency to a particular type of response. Mischel's theory takes into account behavior that might seem inconsistent with a personality, such as the privately shy but publicly extravert singer.

Multiple personalities

According to situationist theories of personality it is possible to possess inconsistent and even contradictory personality traits. Someone who is generally regarded as cold and unemotional, for example, may in certain circumstances display exceptional warmth and empathy. There are cases of "multiple personality disorder" or "dissociative identity disorder," where more than one personality exists in the same person. Such a case, made famous by the book and movie *The Three Faces of Eve*, was described by psychiatrists Corbett H. Thigpen and Hervey M. Cleckley in the 1950s. Their patient Eve described symptoms of headaches and blackouts, but also of discovering evidence of untypical behavior, such as extravagant purchases, of which she had no memory. In therapy, she revealed three distinct personalities, one prim and proper ("Eve White"), another wild and irresponsible ("Eve Black"), and a rational and balanced third ("Jane")—but each was unaware of the others. As Jane, she was introduced to the two "Eves" and helped to integrate them into her own identity.

The psychologists Thigpen and Cleckley helped to write the screenplay for the movie *The Three Faces of Eve.*

Emotions and moods

While personality is often viewed as a stable tendency to behave in a certain way, we also have feelings, moods, and emotions that change in response to our circumstances. Dutch psychologist Nico Frijda explained that we have spontaneous responses to certain situations, which we experience as emotions, but they are also accompanied by physical reactions, such as blushing or hairs standing on end, over which we have no control. As well as the involuntary responses, we have feelings resulting from our conscious thoughts about our emotions, which we experience as moods.

Paul Ekman, another pioneer of the psychology of emotion, noted that one of our involuntary emotional responses is a range of facial expressions. He identified six basic expressions, each associated with primary emotion: anger, fear, disgust, happiness, sadness, and surprise. Like the experience of the emotion itself, these facial expressions are involuntary and impossible to completely control or conceal.

Happiness

Sadness

Surprise

Anger

Disgust

Fear

Many poker players look for "tells" in their opponents, and physical changes under emotional stress are used in lie detection tests and security screening devices.

Which experience comes first—emotional or bodily?

Common sense would suggest that because our emotional responses are involuntary, any action we take comes after our emotion—we run away from a bear, for example, because we are frightened. However, according to many psychologists, this assumption is wrong. William James and Carl Lange proposed that the first response is physical—increased heart rate or trembling—and these actually cause our emotional response. Other studies have shown that physical changes can actually change our emotional responses and the way we feel.

Later psychologists, among them Walter Cannon and Philip Bard, challenged the James–Lange theory, arguing that the physiological and emotional reactions are simultaneous. Richard Lazarus said that we make a cognitive appraisal of a situation that triggers the emotional response. More recently, Robert Zajonc has argued that our thought and emotions are separate processes, and that common sense may be right in assuming that our first response is emotional.

According to Robert Zajonc, emotions seem to skip the thinking part of the brain. Our responses to a frightening situation may involve no cognitive processes.

Normality and abnormality

A perennial problem for psychologists examining individual differences is this: if each of us is a unique individual, is there such a thing as psychological normality or abnormality? Intelligence, for example, is routinely measured as a numerical value—compared with a statistical average (IQ), it carries inevitable connotations of inferiority and superiority. In other areas of the psychology of difference, the measure is less precise, but there are still very often implications of deviation from a "norm" or an ideal. Terms such as "normal" or "abnormal" (and especially the loaded term "subnormal") cannot be truly objective, and reflect society's prejudices about what is acceptable or unacceptable, and desirable or undesirable. There are also strong cultural influences on the definitions of normality and deviance, and also when these individual differences are considered as psychological disorders. A person classed as a harmless eccentric in one culture might be labeled as having a mental disorder in another. The lines between the two—if they exist at all—are far from clear.

Mental disorders

The 20th-century science of psychology emerged from a 19th-century attitude to mental abnormality as an illness requiring medical treatment, the province of psychiatry rather than psychology. This model became increasingly challenged, however, with some psychologists questioning the existence of mental illness altogether (see page 180). Clearly, there are biological causes for some psychological disorders.

This could be actual brain damage through injury, degeneration, or disease—including such things as strokes and Alzheimer's disease or, less obviously, physiological disorders affecting the electrochemical functions of the brain that may be genetic in origin. But there are still many disorders that appear to be purely psychological, for which the label "mental illness" would be inappropriate. Although they may respond to medical treatments, drugs, or surgery, many psychologists have argued that they should be treated as psychological disorders rather than medical illnesses.

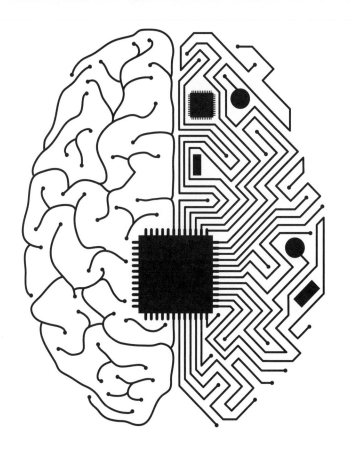

Classification of
mental disorders

It was not until the 19th century that any attempt was made to scientifically identify and classify mental disorders. A founding father of modern psychiatry, Emil Kraepelin believed that serious mental disorders are almost invariably a biological malfunction of the brain, and set out to make a comprehensive list of these, classifying them according to their typical symptoms. Kraepelin found two broad categories of "psychosis" —"dementia praecox" (known as schizophrenia today—see page 16) and manic depression (known as mood disorders). His classification, based on a model of mental illness, formed the basis for almost all subsequent classifications of mental disorders. The two most widely used references currently are the *American Diagnostic and Statistical Manual of Mental Disorders* (DSM), and the relevant section of the *International Statistical Classification of Diseases* (ICD) produced by the World Health Organization, both of which refer to mental disorder rather than illness. Interestingly, definitions in law often lag behind other classifications in this respect.

Here is a list of classified mental disorders:

- Neurodevelopmental disorders
- Schizophrenia spectrum and other psychotic disorders
- Bipolar and related disorders
- Depressive disorders
- Anxiety disorders
- Obsessive-compulsive and related disorders
- Trauma- and stressor-related disorders
- Dissociative disorders
- Somatic symptom disorders
- Feeding and eating disorders
- Elimination disorders
- Sleep-wake disorders
- Sexual dysfunctions
- Gender dysphoria
- Disruptive, impulse control, and conduct disorders
- Substance use and addictive disorders
- Neurocognitive disorders
- Personality disorders
- Paraphilic disorders
- Other disorders

Schizophrenia

Kraepelin's "dementia praecox" (see page 324)—today known as schizophrenia—has remained a major category of serious mental disorder identifiable from a distinctive pattern of symptoms. Contrary to a popular misconception, it is not a "split-personality" disorder. People with schizophrenia may show combinations of many different symptoms, including hearing voices, hallucinations, and problems that affect cognitive functions, such as memory, attention, and decision-making. These affect the ability to function socially and emotionally.

Due to the variety of symptoms and the combinations in which they can be found, schizophrenia is sometimes considered a range of separate disorders rather than a single syndrome. Kraepelin's original classification attributed it to purely biological causes, but since then research into schizophrenia has shown that there are also—as there probably are with a majority of mental disorders—environmental, social, and psychological factors contributing to its onset.

Substance dependence and abuse

One form of "abnormal" behavior that has become a major concern of modern Western society is the use and abuse of psychoactive drugs. These are substances that have a chemical effect on the functions of the brain. They may have a therapeutic use, but their consciousness-altering effects are often pleasurable and they are also used recreationally.

Attitudes to drugs vary from culture to culture, but generally they are seen as a cause of concern once they are perceived as being abused—putting the user or others at risk, or affecting the user's social or professional life—or a user becomes dependent. The term "addiction" is now avoided, not only for its pejorative connotations, but also because it implies dependence is a form of mental illness for which the user holds no responsibility. Dependence can be physical (for example, with heroin or alcohol) or psychological (cannabis, cocaine, or ecstasy, for example) and can cause unpleasant physical or psychological symptoms when a habitual user tries to stop.

Whether certain activities, such as gambling, sex, or using the internet, can be considered addictive is still a matter of debate.

Anxiety disorders

Fear is acknowledged to be one of the fundamental emotions over which we have no control. It is a natural and useful reaction to a threat, but can often be disproportionate to the degree of threat, and can provoke a number of different anxiety disorders. This category of disorder includes phobias, irrational fears of situations or specific objects, but also panic disorders when the fear appears to have no specific stimulus.

A less common, but equally distressing anxiety disorder is obsessive—compulsive disorder (OCD). A person with OCD typically has recurrent, intrusive, and distressing thoughts— the obsessions that cause fear and anxiety. If these thoughts cannot be suppressed or ignored, the sufferer tries to assuage the anxiety with another thought or action, which when repeated becomes a compulsive reaction. Posttraumatic stress disorder (PTSD) is another instance of an anxiety disorder involving intrusive flashbacks to a specific traumatic event, and adversely affecting mood and behavior.

Mood and personality disorders

Originally categorized by Kraepelin as manic-depressive psychosis (see page 324), mood disorders (also known as affective disorders) are the group of mental disorders causing extremes of emotion and mood for prolonged periods of time. At one extreme is the euphoria, energy, and heightened creativity of mania, often accompanied by grandiose ideas and a lack of inhibition; at the other end of the scale is depression, characterized by negativity, sleep problems, and low levels of energy and self-esteem. Depression can often occur on its own, as a "unipolar" disorder (as can mania), but in a minority of cases both are present in a "bipolar" disorder. Sufferers experience prolonged periods of mania or depression, rather than sudden mood swings. Opinion is divided over the causes and treatment of affective disorders. Personality extremes are also classified as mental disorders, especially when they involve aggressive or antisocial tendencies. People who would once be labeled "psychopaths" might now be diagnosed with antisocial personality disorder.

Happiness is not normal

It is possible to see many categories of mental disorder as merely extremes of "normal" behavior, personality, or mood, and abnormal only in the sense that they do not fit society's norms. We tend to focus our attention on negative extremes. To highlight the double standards of our attitudes toward mental "abnormality," Richard Bentall suggested that happiness should be officially classified as a mental disorder, since as a diagnosis of an affective disorder it is as valid as depression.

Bentall suggested that happiness is, "statistically abnormal, consists of a discrete cluster of symptoms, is associated with a range of cognitive abnormalities and probably reflects the abnormal functioning of the central nervous system." Our only reason for not seeking to correct it by treatment is that it is pleasant rather than distressing to the "sufferer" and is valued positively. On a more serious note, Bentall proposed that we should examine our classification of mental disorders to identify any bias that comes from value judgments.

Crazy people?

Several psychologists have questioned the validity of standard classifications of mental disorders. Elliot Aronson said that, "People who do crazy things are not necessarily crazy." In extraordinary circumstances, any of us can act in ways that otherwise would be considered "insane" or irrational. The social psychologists Asch, Milgram, and Zimbardo showed how we are affected by a desire to conform and obey in social situations, even when that behavior seems "crazy" (see pages 200, 208, and 212). Aronson argued that far from being abnormal, sometimes a "crazy" reaction is only natural to come to terms with an exceptional situation, and relieve cognitive dissonance (see page 226). He first noticed this after the shocking events at Kent State University in 1970, where four students were shot dead and several others wounded during a protest. Members of the public and the National Guard justified the actions by making apparently "psychotic" claims about the dissolute lifestyle of the victims, despite their obvious innocence.

Problems in living

Aronson was one of many psychologists to believe that conventional ideas of mental disorder fail to take into account individual circumstances. This in turn raised the question of whether some disorders—especially those classified as mood or anxiety disorders—are in fact perfectly natural reactions of certain individuals to particular situations, and not instances of abnormal behavior.

At the forefront of the critics was psychiatrist Thomas Szasz. He acknowledged that there are a number of disorders that have physiological causes, but in his opinion, too many so-called mental disorders were no more than "problems in living." Categories of mental disorder are a convenient way to marginalize those who have reached the point where their situation exceeds their capacity to deal with it. As an example, Szasz pointed out that the terms "addiction" and "dependence" are often used to stigmatize users of socially unacceptable drugs. Rather than help, we find a label for their incapability.

Many people cope with mood and anxiety disorders as part of "ordinary" life. British wartime prime minister Winston Churchill suffered periods of deep depression, which he called his "black dog."

Telling the difference

In the 1960s, a number of psychologists and psychiatrists rejected the notion of mental illness altogether (see page 180). The feeling behind this antipsychiatry movement was that medicalization of mental disorders is a form of social manipulation that threatens individual liberties and human rights. Others objected on different grounds. Richard Bentall, for example, argued that there is no clear line dividing the mentally healthy and unhealthy. Instead, there is a continuum, which includes extremes of mood, behavior, and personality, and we all fall somewhere on it. Rather than considering psychotic symptoms, such as hearing voices, as abnormal, he suggested that we all experience something similar to a greater or lesser extent. David Rosenhan, took yet another critical view—the fact that psychiatric diagnosis is made according to the classification of symptoms was, in his view, hopelessly unreliable. His researchers presented themselves to mental institutions and were misdiagnosed with mental disorders by psychiatrists who also failed to diagnose genuine patients.

Clinical psychology

Probably the most widespread application of psychological theory is in the treatment of mental disorders. In the first half of the 20th century treatment of psychological disorders—psychotherapy—was dominated by two very different approaches: the psychiatric, or medical approach, and the Freudian psychoanalytical approach. Discoveries in neuroscience and the theories of experimental psychology, however, influenced thinking in psychiatry and the emerging field of clinical psychology. Modern forms of psychotherapy evolved from Freud's idea of a "talking cure," but the ideas of behaviorism and cognitive and social psychology have gradually taken the place of his psychodynamic theory. Psychiatry, too, has been influenced by psychological theory, moving from the medical model of mental disorders as symptoms of physical illness to an appreciation of the psychological factors involved. Advances in neuroscience have also shed some light on the connections between its physiological workings and our psychological problems.

Psychology Room
1

Do not disturb

Clinical psychology is a distinct branch of psychology, drawing on ideas and discoveries from all other fields of research.

Psychiatry vs. psychology

Psychiatry is distinguished from psychology as it is a branch of medicine as opposed to a branch of science. Psychiatry's approach to treatment has traditionally been based on the idea that mental disorders are illnesses with primarily biological causes, requiring medical treatment with drugs or surgery. Psychologists, by contrast, generally regard mental disorders as having psychological causes, which require treating by therapy. In practice, of course, the line between the two is not so clear-cut. Many psychiatrists are trained psychoanalysts (Freud himself was originally a medical doctor, specializing in neurology and psychiatry), or have studied experimental and biological psychology. Clinical psychologists, equally, are often well informed about medical, psychiatric treatments, as well as current thinking in neuroscience and experimental psychology. Increasingly, treatments are not so easily divided along psychiatric/psychological and medicine/psychotherapy lines, and mental disorders are often treated with a combination of medical and psychological techniques.

PSYCHIATRY	PSYCHOLOGY
medical	mental disorders
mental illness	problems in living
doctor	psychotherapist
physiological	talking cure
neuroscience	psychoanalysis
drugs and surgery	counseling

Treatments and therapies

Treatment of mental disorders evolved along two lines. In the mid-19th century, attitudes toward "insanity" were shifting, and the idea that mental problems are a disease or inherited impairment prompted the establishment of psychiatry as a branch of medicine. Since mental disorders were considered to be caused by physical malfunctions of the brain, it seemed obvious to treat them physically with surgery or drugs. Meanwhile, Freud and others were developing less invasive, psychological treatments.

There has since been much cross-fertilization between the two approaches, as well as influence from experimental psychology and neuroscience. While they may disagree about the ultimate cause of mental disorders, psychologists acknowledge that physical treatments have often proved effective in alleviating the psychological symptoms of many disorders, and psychiatrists recognize the success of treatments such as cognitive-behavioral therapy.

Physical treatments

Damage to different parts of the brain, or interference with the electrochemical communication between brain cells, can affect cognitive functions, moods, personality, and behavior. Sometimes, however, a positive, therapeutic effect can be achieved surgically, by removing or "disconnecting" an "unhealthy" part of the brain. This once-common treatment for serious psychosis is viewed with suspicion nowadays. Similarly controversial is electroconvulsive therapy (ECT), which can be effective in cases of severe depression using electric shocks to alter neural communications. Psychoactive drugs work more subtly, altering brain chemistry to enhance or impair particular neural connections. However, drug treatments can also cause unwanted cognitive impairment and carry the risk of dependence. Yet, while some psychologists challenge the wisdom of physical therapies, control groups given placebos in clinical drug trials often show marked improvement compared to those given no treatment. This placebo effect shows the potential for psychological treatment of physical symptoms.

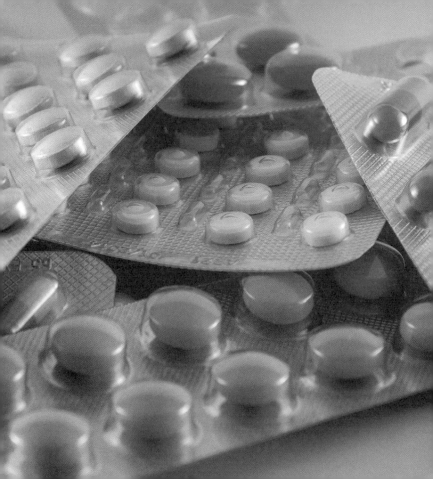

Psychoanalysis and psychotherapy

An alternative to physical treatment of mental disorders evolved from the work of neurologists, such as Jean-Martin Charcot, and their interest in the effects of hypnosis. This work strongly influenced the neurologist and psychiatrist Sigmund Freud (right), who saw the root cause of neurotic disorders as inner conflict between the conscious and unconscious parts of the psyche (see page 146) rather than physical malfunction. Treatment would help patients find insight into their condition through psychoanalysis.

Numerous different versions of a "talking cure" (see page 144) evolved from Freud's model, some developments of his psychodynamic approach, others as a reaction against it. Different methods of psychotherapy were based on schools of thought in other branches of psychology, such as behaviorism (see page 46), Gestalt psychology (see page 110), and cognitive psychology (see page 90), but all had in common the basic idea of using psychology instead of physical treatments.

Criticism of psychoanalysis

Throughout the 20th century, a range of different forms of psychotherapy emerged—many radically different to Freud's psychodynamic theory. Despite these developments, psychoanalysis remained the predominant psychological approach in clinical psychology until the 1950s, when a number of psychologists proposed alternative explanations. They also openly criticized and even discredited psychoanalysis as a form of therapy. Freud's theories were denounced as unscientific, with most criticism leveled at the lack of objective evidence of any improvement in patients' conditions after psychoanalysis.

In 1952, Hans Eysenck launched a searing attack on Freudian theory, citing his study where patients showed no more improvement than if they had no treatment at all. Aaron Beck, influenced by Albert Ellis' rejection of Freudian analysis, produced similar evidence disputing the claims of psychoanalysis. Beck had practiced as a psychoanalyst, but felt it was more a matter of faith than scientific theory.

If the truth
contradicts
deeply held
beliefs,
that is too bad.

Hans Eysenck

Humanistic psychology

One of the reactions against Freudian psychoanalysis came from the growing movement of humanistic psychology in the mid-20th century. Psychodynamic theory emphasized the primal drives we all experience, and the inner conflict produced when they are inhibited by the ego and superego. Humanist psychology turned attention to the individual person and his or her ability to satisfy a whole range of needs.

American psychotherapist Abraham Maslow (see pages 44 and 170) was at the forefront of the humanist movement in clinical psychology. He recognized that both behavior and psychological well-being are shaped by satisfaction of "higher" social and personal needs, and realization of personal goals. At these higher levels of need we seek fulfillment, rather than simply satisfaction, and a sense of achieving potential. Humanistic psychotherapy focuses on helping people identify a purpose and meaning in life and resolve inner turmoil by meeting a full range of personal needs.

Hierarchy of human needs

Our needs, according to Maslow, are what motivate us to do things, to fulfill our purpose in life. How well we succeed in satisfying those needs determines how we feel about ourselves and affects our outlook on the world. Maslow identified many different kinds of need, ranging from the purely physical necessities of survival, through social relationships, to more "spiritual" needs of personal growth. He presented them as a pyramidal hierarchy, with physiological needs (air, food, water, and sleep) at the bottom and above these, other survival needs (security, shelter, and money). Next come social needs (loving relationships, sexual intimacy, friendship, and acceptance in a social group) and then the more personal needs of self-esteem. The next step is the first of Maslow's "higher" needs—the things we seek out for personal growth and realization of potential. These range from a cognitive need to acquire knowledge, the aesthetic need to appreciate beauty, and the need to achieve personal potential. At the top is self-transcendence, acting for things beyond ourselves.

Self-transcendence needs	Helping others to achieve self-actualization
Self-actualization needs	Realizing personal potential, self-fulfillment, seeking personal growth, and peak experiences
Aesthetic needs	Appreciation and search for beauty, balance, form, etc.
Cognitive needs	Knowledge, meaning, etc.
Esteem needs	Self-esteem, achievement, mastery, independence, status, dominance, prestige, etc.
Social needs	Belonging and love—family, friendship, work group, sexual intimacy, etc.
Safety needs	Protection from the elements, security, order, law, stability, etc.
Biological and physiological needs	Air, food, drink, shelter, warmth, sex, sleep etc.

Person-centered therapy

Humanistic psychology led several psychologists to question the approach of traditional psychotherapy. In the 1960s, Carl Rogers challenged the fundamental assumptions of clinical psychology, suggesting that therapy should be centered on the person rather than the disorder. The path to mental health, in his view, is for the individual to discover his or her own "good life." The patient should avoid attempting to fit into a preconceived idea of the person he or she should be, or the life he or she should lead. The good life is not the end product of a course of therapy but rather a continuing process.

To achieve this, Rogers explained, we need to live in the present, without reliving past satisfactions or disappointments. If we are open to experience the world as it is, we will be able to see a multitude of possibilities. People are essentially good and healthy, so we must take the perspective of "unconditional positive regard" for both ourselves and other people, and trust our judgment to make positive choices.

Behavioral therapy

Joseph Wolpe, a South African pioneer of behavioral therapy, was one of the first psychologists to challenge the effectiveness of traditional psychotherapy. In the Second World War he served in the army as a medical officer, and treated men returning from active duty with "war neurosis." Using the standard method of encouraging the men to talk about their experiences, Wolpe found it was far from effective, and lost faith in traditional psychoanalytical techniques.

He turned instead to behaviorist theory (see page 46), and the idea that some form of conditioning could be used in treatment of mental disorders. Teaching relaxation techniques to soldiers suffering from posttraumatic stress disorder (PTSD) allowed them to manage their anxiety. Wolpe reasoned that in disorders such as PTSD, anxiety resulted from fear —an emotional response to a stimulus. By conditioning, that response could be unlearned, or at least altered, and replaced by another emotional response that would induce relaxation.

Reciprocal inhibition

Long before Wolpe's proposal of conditioning as a technique of behavioral psychotherapy, behaviorist psychologists had advocated its use as a means of modifying behavior —encouraging "desirable," and discouraging "undesirable" behavior. This kind of behavior modification formed the basis for a form of behavioral therapy suggested by B.F. Skinner (see page 72), among others. But what Wolpe was suggesting was something different: using conditioning to modify not behavior but emotional response, in a process known as reciprocal inhibition. The idea was a simple one. The Little Albert experiment (see page 60) showed that an emotional response could be learned using classical Pavlovian conditioning, and could also be unlearned. From his experience with PTSD sufferers, Wolpe knew that it is impossible to feel two conflicting emotions simultaneously, such as fear and relaxation. If a patient is conditioned to respond to a stimulus with a feeling of calm, this inhibits the fearful response that causes anxiety.

Assertiveness training can help people to modify their behavior to overcome stage fright or anxiety in social situations.

Systematic desensitization

Wolpe went on from his technique of reciprocal inhibition (see page 362) to develop other methods of behavioral therapy. The best known is systematic desensitization, also called graduated exposure therapy, which has proved effective in the treatment of phobias and other anxiety disorders. Again the idea was simple—a person can unlearn a fearful response to an anxiety-producing stimulus by gradually increased levels of exposure to it, overcoming fear by degrees. Wolpe suggested it could be done in three steps. The patient first identifies the things that cause an anxiety, for example phobia of spiders, and arranges them into a hierarchy according to the severity of anxiety that they provoke—looking at pictures of spiders, seeing a dead spider, seeing a live spider, touching a spider, holding a spider, and so on. Next, he or she learns relaxation and coping techniques. Then, he or she is exposed to the lowest-ranked anxiety stimulus and practices applying coping techniques. Once that fear has been mastered, the patient moves onto the next level and gradually overcomes anxiety.

Aversion therapy

The concept of conditioning inspired several different forms of behavior therapy. Some relied on a variety of different methods of behavior modification, generally to discourage a specific behavior considered undesirable. Among these is aversion therapy, a treatment that relies on the principle of negative reinforcement (see page 76), and was originally developed for use in treating addictions and unwanted habits.

In essence, it is a process of conditioning in which a person learns to associate a particular behavior with unpleasant or uncomfortable sensations—for example, the habit of nail-biting can be broken by painting the nails with a bitter-tasting substance. The negative reinforcement for more serious cases of habitual or addictive behavior tend to be correspondingly severe, such as adding chemicals with nasty side effects into alcoholic drinks. The ethics of some forms of aversion therapy is questionable, and actual physical discomfort has largely been replaced with imagined, or "covert," aversion.

In Anthony Burgess' *A Clockwork Orange*, the main character is given a nausea-inducing drug and forced to view graphic images, in an attempt to cure his violent tendencies.

Rational emotive behavior therapy

After the Second World War, behaviorist ideas began to be replaced by cognitive psychology, and psychotherapists turned their attention to the role of cognitive processes in emotional disorders and their treatment. Among the first of these was Albert Ellis, who had initially trained as a Freudian psychoanalyst. Influenced by the "cognitive revolution" in the 1950s, he developed rational emotive behavior therapy (REBT).

He believed that mood disorders are not so much the response to a negative event, as brought about by the way we view that event—our rational or irrational beliefs about it. When something negative happens—the "activating event"—we might have an automatic negative emotional response, which simply confirms our belief that the event is negative and we can fall into a spiral of negativity. Alternatively, we can choose to make a less emotional and more rational response to the negative event, and this puts the event into perspective and avoids reinforcing self-damaging negative emotions.

The ABCs of REBT

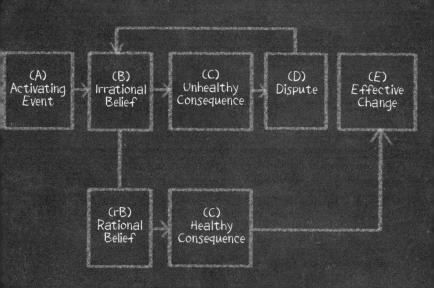

A cognitive approach

With postwar cognitive psychology came a demand for even stricter scientific methodology, and psychoanalysis was subjected in several studies to scientific scrutiny. Aaron Beck was one of a number of psychoanalysts who became disillusioned with psychodynamic methods of therapy at this time, shifting his attention from what he saw as unscientific theories of the unconscious to cognitive processes.

Like Ellis, he felt that mood disorders are caused by negative thoughts, and the key to an effective treatment is to help the patient to recognize and understand irrational ways of thinking. He applied this method to treating cases of depression, which he believed resulted from what he called the "cognitive triad"—three negative beliefs about the self, the world or environment, and the future. These form a vicious circle, leading from the thought, "I am worthless" and around and around again to "I am worthless because I never can be any good."

Negative views about oneself

"I am worthless"

Negative views about the world

"Everything goes wrong because I am worthless"

Negative views about the future

"I'll never be any good because everything always goes wrong"

Cognitive–behavioral therapy

Beck developed a way of breaking the vicious circle of negative thoughts that lead to depression by getting patients to think about them rationally. This process changes the way a situation is viewed and helps to show that things are seldom wholly negative or positive. Initially, Beck's therapy consisted solely of a cognitive appraisal of negative thoughts, and was known as cognitive therapy. But he was open to all sorts of ideas, so long as they could be proved effective scientifically, and became interested in some of the methods of behavioral therapy. These he incorporated into his treatments to become what is now called cognitive–behavioral therapy (CBT). This typically progresses in two stages: first a patient identifies the irrational, negative thoughts that are the cause of his or her emotional distress, and compares these beliefs with objective facts about the situation to gain a different perspective. Then some form of behavior modification can be used to discourage actions that reinforce those negative thoughts.

Physicality
Heart racing, sweating, nervous twitch, hand wringing

Emotions
Anxious, sad, stressed

Thoughts
Worried, negative, frightened

Behavior
Become aggressive or more tentative, snap at people, avoid social occasions

Automatic thoughts

In Beck's cognitive theory of depression, he described the triad of irrational negative beliefs as "automatic thoughts." As well as being a cause of depression, these automatic thoughts are central to other mood and anxiety disorders, in particular obsessive-compulsive disorder (OCD). In OCD, the obsession manifests itself as automatic thoughts that produce feelings of fear, discomfort, and apprehension that are extremely distressing, and often connected with death and disease, or unpleasant and embarrassing ideas of a sexual nature.

These thoughts are not only irrational, but also intrusive and recurrent, and cannot simply be ignored or denied. The obsession is often accompanied by an equally irrational belief that certain behavior will prevent or reduce the anxiety, for example hand-washing or rituals such as counting. These behaviors also become impossible to control, or compulsive, and as recurrent and repetitive as the obsessive anxiety they are believed to relieve. OCD, however, responds well to CBT.

Learned helplessness theory

Beck's cognitive theory of depression broke the mold of thinking about mood disorders, introducing the idea that we can stop the spiral of negativity by consciously changing perceptions. Further research into the causes of depression were conducted by psychologists including Martin Seligman, who described this spiral as the result of "learned helplessness."

He had found in experiments with animals that, when repeatedly subjected to unpleasant or painful stimuli that they could not avoid, they do not take the opportunity to avoid discomfort, even when they are given it. Seligman concluded that they had learned that they have no control over the situation. Similarly, people who experience negative thoughts learn to perceive them as being beyond their control, and feel they are helpless to influence the outcome of a situation. By understanding depression as stemming from both irrational negative thoughts and learned helplessness, it can effectively be treated with the two-pronged approach of CBT.

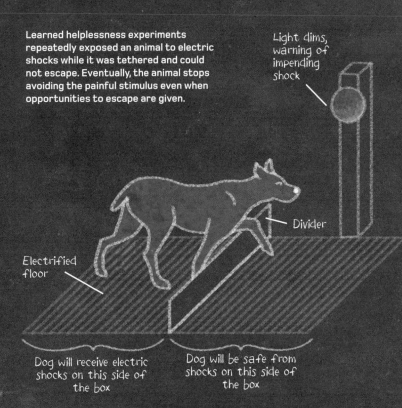

Learned helplessness experiments repeatedly exposed an animal to electric shocks while it was tethered and could not escape. Eventually, the animal stops avoiding the painful stimulus even when opportunities to escape are given.

Light dims, warning of impending shock

Divider

Electrified floor

Dog will receive electric shocks on this side of the box

Dog will be safe from shocks on this side of the box

Positive psychology

Learned helplessness theory was the result of many years of research into depression, which had a personal significance for Seligman, who came to realize he himself was prone to negativity and depression. He was persuaded to follow his own advice and change his perceptions of the situation. In this, he was influenced by the ideas of humanistic psychologists, especially Albert Ellis's approach to psychotherapy (see page 368). Seligman agreed that clinical psychology puts too much emphasis on the negative—disorders and their treatment—rather than encouraging positive thinking about what allows us a good, healthy, and happy life. This became the "positive psychology" movement. Ellis began to study those who are happy to try to identify what makes a happy life. He found that there is no single recipe for happiness, but that there are three different kinds of happy life: the "Pleasant Life," based on socializing and sensual pleasures; the "Meaningful Life," found by working for something beyond oneself; and the "Good Life," achieved by fulfilling one's potential for personal growth.

The flow

One of the aspects of positive psychology identified by Seligman as important to a good and happy life is a sense of satisfaction and achievement. This can be more than just the satisfied feeling of a job well done. It was psychologist Mihály Csíkszentmihályi who coined the term "the flow" to describe the state of absorption we experience when totally engaged with a task.

Completely losing yourself in what you are doing, or finding "the flow," is more a state of ecstasy than simple happiness or contentment. This is not just something that we enjoy doing, but also an activity that challenges us enough to require our absolute concentration. We can then find that we are no longer conscious of ourselves or what is happening around us, and enter a different state of consciousness, where although we are completely focused on what we are doing, we feel a sense of calm and timelessness, and achieve an inner clarity of living in the moment.

Mindfulness and meditation

Methods of psychotherapy have sometimes been influenced from outside mainstream psychology altogether, in particular the meditative practices associated with several Asian religions. Interest in exotic cultures came with the hippies of the 1960s and continued with "New Age" ideas. At the same time, elements of Indian traditional culture, including the yogic practices of Hinduism and Buddhism, became integrated into Western popular culture.

Yoga and meditation became recognized at first as relaxation techniques, but some psychologists realized that these methods also help practitioners to achieve a "mindfulness" that allows them to calmly observe their own thought processes as if from the outside. Because this is a detached and nonjudgmental view, it can be used in cognitive therapies to identify the negative thoughts that may be causing mood disorders such as depression, and change perception of their emotional significance.

The relevance of psychology

Psychology established itself as a distinct branch of science less than 150 years ago but has become a significant part of modern culture. Psychological theories are part of mainstream thought, and terms such as "inferiority complex" and "OCD" a part of our everyday language. In short, psychology influences all our lives, changing the way we think about ourselves and other people, and helping to shape our modern societies.

Applications for psychology are equally ubiquitous, since aspects of our behavior and cognitive processes are involved in all our activities. But only a minority of trained psychologists take up research careers and come up with theories; most find posts where theory is put into practice, and psychologists can be employed in almost every walk of life. Unsurprisingly, many work in the closely related areas of mental health and education, but others also take on less obvious roles in business and industry, advertising and the media, sports and entertainment, the law and politics, and even economics.

Clinical and health psychology

The most obvious application of psychological theories and discoveries is in the field of clinical psychology. Here, psychologists train in a variety of therapies to treat mental disorders, or more generally to work in all aspects of mental healthcare. As well as treatment of the disorders themselves, this may involve assessment of the impact they have on the patient's social and personal life, including his or her ability to deal with responsibilities and hold down a job, and the knock-on effects on other people such as family, friends, and colleagues.

Mental disorders may also affect physical health, and involve a collaboration of different healthcare professionals. The other side of the coin is the realm of health psychology, which among other things helps patients to deal with the psychological effects of physical illness or injury. Although generally not medically trained, psychologists working in the fields of mental health are often attached to a hospital or healthcare center, and work alongside doctors and nurses.

Counseling and guidance

It is not just when coping with specific mental disorders, such as depression or anxiety, that we may need the support of a professional psychologist. We all go through periods of stress at various stages in our lives, which can take a toll on our mental well-being. These may be the "rites of passage" that are a normal and natural part of progressing through life, or hurdles, which may require difficult decisions. Bereavement and divorce, for example, can be painful and difficult to cope with alone.

A negative reaction to stressful events is not abnormal, and does not usually require psychotherapy or treatment, but rather the guidance of a counselor. Counselors are trained in the various different psychological strains we may encounter, from problems at school to choosing a career, marital and family problems, the effects of substance abuse, to bereavement, dealing with disability, and terminal illness. They help their clients to develop strategies to cope with negative situations and maintain a psychologically healthy life.

Criminal psychology

In popular fiction, forensic psychologists are often profilers, helping to track down psychopathic killers from clues of their personality, or advising police on how to negotiate with a kidnapper or hostage-taker. But this is only a very small part of the wide field of psychology and the law. There is a great deal of research into mental disorders that lead to criminal and antisocial behavior, which involve not only psychopathology but also aspects of social and personality psychology.

Much of this study centers on convicted criminals in prisons, and criminological psychologists also work with prisoners to help with their rehabilitation. Psychology plays a significant role in courts of law, too, with expert witnesses being called upon to give evidence or help decide the degree of responsibility of a defendant, or the reliability of eyewitness testimony (see page 136). Behind the scenes, psychologists may determine ages of consent and criminal responsibility, for example, or what mental disorders should come under the jurisdiction of the courts.

Organizational psychology

Ideas from social psychology have had an enormous impact on the way we organize ourselves in groups of all kinds, from small social groups to the wider community, and work together toward common goals. An understanding of the roles of individual members of the group and the forces that bring them together is especially useful for encouraging "team spirit" in business and industry where the members of an organization need to work together, drawing on individual skills and abilities, and establishing a chain of command.

The same principles apply in other forms of institution, too, and theories of group dynamics and group coherence can be used to ensure the unity of organizations, such as political parties or religious groups with a shared belief or common interest. As well as the internal dynamics and structure of an organization, social psychology can shed light on its relationship and interactions with other organizations, and its place in the wider community.

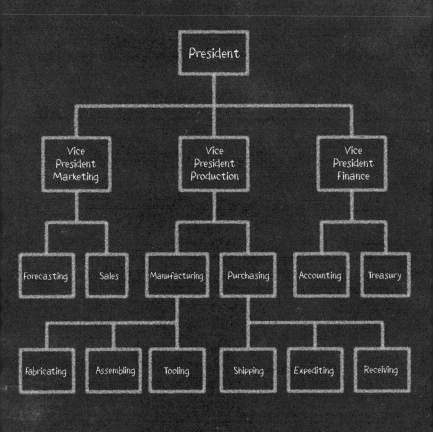

Advertising and
the media

Research into attitudes and methods of persuasion has an obvious relevance to the world of advertising and marketing, not only providing advertisers with techniques to persuade people to buy their products, but also targeting their campaigns effectively. Questionnaires and surveys developed to assess attitudes in psychological studies, for example, have been adopted to gauge the markets for products and choose the most appropriate means of promoting them.

Certain tricks of the trade, such as professional or celebrity endorsement, and emotional and sex appeal, all have their basis in psychological theories. Ideas can be sold in the same way as products, in propaganda, political campaigns, or even religious evangelizing, often playing on fears and prejudices rather than presenting rational arguments—a technique backed up by psychological studies. These methods of persuasion can also be used more positively and prosocially—for example, in public health campaigns, health and safety, and charitable issues.

Butlin's

FOR YOUR HOLIDAY

FREE
BOOKLET
Send P.C. to
BUTLIN'S LTD.
(Dept. H.B.)
439, OXFORD ST
LONDON, W.I.

Education

Developmental psychology turned educational theory on its head by focusing not on teaching but on learning. Jean Piaget (see page 250) and other psychologists showed that children go through various stages of cognitive development, and undergo a different process of exploration and discovery in each stage. The role of the educator is not to impose information or instruction, but to guide learning. Psychology also showed that students learn best by hands-on experience, too, and not from "book learning."

These ideas were adopted by many educational establishments in Europe and the USA, influencing a major overhaul of curriculum design and teaching practice, with a focus on progressively expanding areas of study to match the stages of a child's development. Traditional ideas of rote learning have persisted, however, and are still championed by some conservative educationalists. Depending on a government's stance on education, psychologists may advise on policy.

Management and human resources

Almost every aspect of social psychology has some relevance to the way that business organizations function effectively. Studies of social groups have shown how hierarchies develop and members are allotted positions within them, according to their strengths and weaknesses. Leaders emerge or are appointed, and it is their role to encourage group cohesion, assess the needs of the organization and its individual members, and strike a balance between the two. Being a good boss is more than simply ensuring everyone does their job, and involves an understanding of the underlying psychology. Human resource management, perhaps even more than leadership, is reliant on social psychology principles. Its role includes ensuring that individual members feel that their contribution is worthwhile and appreciated, and that pressures within and outside the organization do not affect their work. Techniques of persuasion and an understanding of attitudes and "ingroups" are also vital in industrial relations, to ensure that disputes can be quickly and amicably resolved.

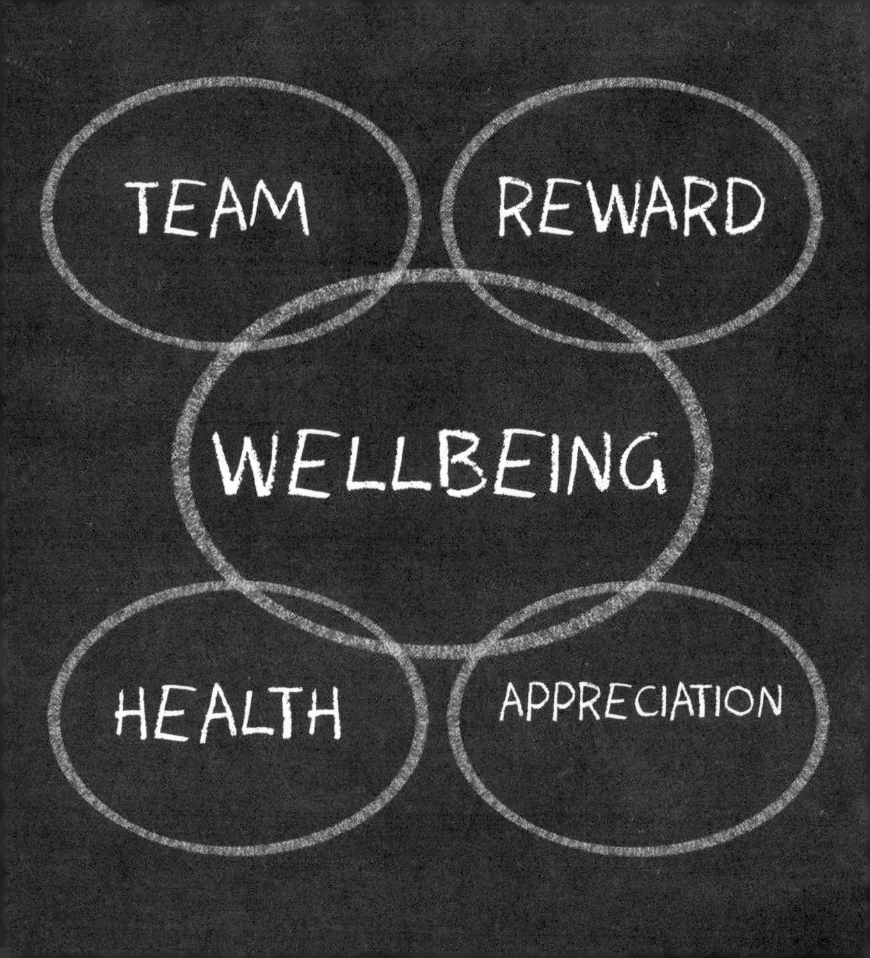
TEAM
REWARD
WELLBEING
HEALTH
APPRECIATION

Occupational psychology

While social psychology provides a framework for organizations and an efficient management structure, it is cognitive psychology that has done most to improve the conditions of the workforce. Understanding cognitive processes, such as attention, and the effects of physical and psychological stress, has led to radical change in working practices, especially in manufacturing industries. Repetitive and sometimes dangerous work on production lines in noisy, overheated factories was shown to be bad not only for workers' health, safety, and morale, but also for productivity.

Donald Broadbent promoted the idea that the purpose of psychology is to solve real-life problems. Manufacturing was not the only industry to benefit from cognitive psychology—psychologists have studied the range of cognitive skills needed in almost every kind of job, and how workplace conditions and working practices can be improved to make them more pleasant and productive, for both businesses and the workers.

Sports psychology

The psychology of social groups is particularly relevant to team sports, where "team spirit" is an important factor in successful performance on the field. The idea of competition between teams is also related to notions of "ingroups" and "outgroups" (see page 204), and a good coach or manager of a team will understand which elements of groupthink can be used positively to ensure a healthy competitive attitude.

Solo sports people turn to social psychology, too. The element of competition undoubtedly inspires them to perform, but psychologists have shown the simple presence of another person can enhance performance, leading many sports people to train with others (see page 188). Athletes and cyclists, for example, regularly use pacesetters. Studies of teams have also highlighted the dangers of social loafing (see page 190), or conflict within the team, resulting from a feeling that the contributions of the players are not valued equally, or are not fairly distributed.

Psychology today and tomorrow

As with any science, we can never discover all there is to know about psychology. Theories seldom offer complete explanations and are often contradicted by new theories. However, the interface of psychology with other disciplines is receiving the greatest interest at the present. Advances in neuroscience, for example, have helped toward a better understanding of the elusive concept of consciousness, and the interaction of computer sciences and psychology has accelerated developments in artificial intelligence.

New applications for psychological theories are also being discovered, most obviously in clinical psychology, where techniques for diagnosing and treating mental disorders continue to be developed, but also in business and industry. Psychologist Daniel Kahneman shared a Nobel Memorial Prize in economics, and global economic, social, and political turbulence in recent years only serves to highlight the importance of new fields of human psychology.

Pop psychology

For as long as philosophers and scientists have attempted to explain the human mind and human behavior, their ideas have been reported, discussed, and presented to an eager public. Popular psychology may seem a comparatively recent phenomenon, but books such as Robert Burton's 1621 *The Anatomy of Melancholy* were bestsellers of their time. Many psychologists, from Freud to Kahneman, have become household names, and Milgram's and Zimbardo's experiments (see pages 208 and 212) are equally well known.

Our fascination with what makes us (and other people) tick goes beyond a desire to understand or for self-improvement, and is a perennial source of entertainment in fiction and drama. Reality TV presents psychological situations as much for entertainment as information. Humans are naturally inquisitive and one of their favorite subjects is themselves. This is why psychology—the study of mind and human behavior—has always been one of the most popular of the sciences.

Glossary

Archetype
In Jung's theory of the collective unconscious, an image or idea that has a universal meaning

Attachment
A strong emotional bond, such as between a child and its mother

Attitude
A tendency to respond to things, ideas, and people in a certain way, shaped by beliefs and values

Behaviorism
The approach to psychology that studies observable behavior rather than mental processes

Circadian rhythm
The pattern of daily activity determined by our "body clock"

Classical conditioning
A type of learning in which a conditioned response becomes triggered by a neutral stimulus

Cognitive
Concerned with mental processes including memory, perception, consciousness, and reasoning

Cognitive dissonance
The discomfort a person feels when holding two conflicting beliefs, or when the facts contradict a deeply held belief

Cognitive psychology
The approach to psychology that studies mental processes rather than behavior

Collective unconscious
In Jung's theory, the part of the psyche containing inherited ideas and images, the archetypes

Conditioning
Any of several types of learning where a response becomes associated with a stimulus

Consciousness
An awareness of oneself, one's thoughts, and environment

Crystallized intelligence
The ability to use knowledge and skills that have been learned through education and experience

Drive
The biological needs that motivate us to satisfy physiological needs

Developmental psychology
Branch of psychology concerned with stages of growth, and interaction between physical and psychological processes

Ego
In Freud's theory, the conscious, rational part of the psyche that moderates the promptings of the id

Episodic memory
Memory of events, as opposed to semantic memory or procedural memory

Extravert
A personality type that is directed toward the outside world

Fluid intelligence
The ability to solve new problems without using learned knowledge or skills

FMRI (functional MRI)
A brain imaging technique that detects magnetic changes in the flow of blood to cells in the brain

Gender
The psychological, rather than physiological, state of maleness or femaleness

General intelligence (g)
According to Spearman, the factor that underlies all intelligent behavior

Gestalt psychology
An approach that maintains that all aspects of psychology should be considered as a whole, rather than individual constituent parts

Gestalt therapy
A form of psycho-therapy that focuses on the whole person

Groupthink
A tendency of groups to sometimes value conformity more than rational decision-making

Heuristics
"Rules of thumb" that we use as shortcuts in preference to rational thinking in complex problems

Id
In Freud's theory, the unconscious part of the psyche that pursues pleasure and satisfaction impulsively and instinctively

Imprinting
In some animals, the process of forming an attachment to the first moving thing they encounter

Instinct
An inborn and inherited tendency to a particular behavior, usually necessary for survival

Introvert
A personality type that is directed inward, toward itself

**IQ
(Intelligence quotient)**
A measure of general intelligence as compared with the average (an IQ of 100) of the population as a whole

Long-term memory (LTM)
The memory processes for storing information and retrieving it at a later time

Neuron
A cell in the nervous system that can receive and/or transmit electrochemical signals

Neuroscience
The study of the brain and central nervous system

Operant conditioning
A type of conditioning in which an organism learns behavior through observing the effect its actions have on its environment

Perception
The cognitive process of interpreting information from the senses to make sense of the external world

Placebo
A substance that has no therapeutic effect, used as a control in testing drugs

Procedural memory
Memory of skills and abilities, how to do things, as opposed to episodic memory or semantic memory

Psychiatry
The branch of medicine dealing with mental illness

Psychoanalysis
The form of psychotherapy originally developed by Freud to uncover unconscious conflicts and drives that cause mental disorders

Psychodynamics
In Freud's theory, the sometimes conflicting forces between different parts of the psyche

Psychotherapy
Any of a number of different methods of treating mental disorders using psychological theories rather than drugs or surgery

Reinforcement
In conditioning, anything that increases the probability of a response

Repression
In Freud's theory, the way the psyche deals with uncomfortable ideas and memories by removing them from the conscious mind and pushing them deep into the unconscious

Schizophrenia
A group of severe mental disorders characterized by impairment of mental functions and a a distorted perception of reality. Symptoms can include hallucinations, and disturbed behavior, emotions, and personality

Semantic memory
Memory of facts and knowledge, as opposed to episodic memory or procedural memory

Short-term memory (STM)
Memory processes for dealing with information needed for a specific task, not needing to be stored in long-term memory

Stooge (aka confederate)
A person who takes part in a psychological experiment pretending to be a subject but is in fact working for the researcher

Superego
In Freud's theory, the part of the psyche that upholds the standards and morals learn from parents, society, and authority

Synaptic transmission
The electrochemical transmission of information from one neuron to another across the synapse, the gap between them

Traits
The various qualities and attributes that combine to form our personalities

Unconscious
In psychoanalysis, the larger part of the psyche where our primitive urges and repressed memories are stored

Index

$1 or $20 experiment 230

Adler, Alfred 142, 165
adolescence 276
advertising 394
"ages of me" 284
aggression 216
Ainsworth, Mary 242, 244
Albert B experiment 60, 66
Allport, Floyd 188, 304, 312
altruism 218
analysis 154, 184
animal experimentation 80
antipsychiatry movement
    182, 340
antisocial behavior 216
anxiety disorders 330, 364
archetypes 162
Aronson, Eliot 336, 338
Asch, Solomon 198, 200, 202
attachment theory 240–8
attention 124, 126
attitudes 222
attraction, interpersonal
    232–3
automatic thoughts 374
aversion therapy 366–7

Baby X experiments 274
Baddeley, Alan 132

Bandura, Albert 216, 266,
    268
Beck, Aaron 352, 370–4, 372
behavioral therapy 360–9
behaviorism 20, 46–88
Behaviorist Manifesto 58
Bentall, Richard 334, 340
Berkowitz, Leonard 216
Berne, Eric 184
Bettelheim, Bruno 248
Binet, Alfred 287
biological psychology 22,
    24–45
blank slate 62
Bobo doll experiment 268–9
Bower, Gordon H. 132
Bowlby, John 240, 242, 246
brain 26–32, 102–3
brain damage 34–5
Broadbent, Donald 118, 124,
    126, 128, 400
Broca's area 32, 34
Bruner, Jerome 118, 260
bystander effect 219

Cattell, Raymond 296
Charcot, Jean-Martin 14, 16
Cherry, Colin 126, 129
"child as apprentice" 258
child development, and

psychoanalysis 166–8
"child as scientist" 256, 258
Chomsky, Noam 104
chunking 122–3
clinical psychology 342–82,
    386, 404
cocktail party effect 126–7,
    129
cognitive-behavioral
    therapy (CBT) 372–4
cognitive behaviorism 68–9
cognitive development,
    stages of 252–8
cognitive dissonance 226,
    228, 230, 336
cognitive psychology
    90–140, 262, 368, 370, 400
collective unconscious 160
conditioning 20, 46, 52, 58,
    60, 104, 360, 366
    classical 50–1, 70, 74, 82,
    362
    operant 74–5, 76, 78, 82, 88
    positive and negative 54–5
conformity 198, 200, 202,
    206, 214
consciousness 36–7, 38
counseling 388
Crick, Francis 38
criminal psychology 390

Cᴅikszentmihályi, Mihály 380

cultural development 260–1

Darley, John 220
decision-making 140
depression 332, 370, 370–6, 372
developmental psychology 236–84
difference, psychology of 286–340
dreams/dream analysis 158–9
drives 44, 148–9
drug abuse 328

Ebbinghaus, Hermann 90–8, 130
education 256, 396
ego 146, 147, 172
Ekman, Paul 316
electric shock experiments 206, 208–9, 210
electroconvulsive therapy (ECT) 348
Ellis, Albert 368, 378
emotions 316–18
Erikson, Erik 262, 276, 278, 280
ethics, experimental 66
eugenics 62, 294
existential psychotherapy 174
eye 31

eyewitness testimony 136, 390
Eysenck, Hans 306, 308, 352

faces, recognizing 116–17
False Self 168
Festinger, Leon 226, 228, 230
field theory 194–5
filter models 128–9
flow, the 380
forgetting 96–7, 134
Frankl, Viktor 172
free association 154, 156–7
Freud, Sigmund 14, 22, 136, 142, 144–58, 262, 302, 342, 344, 350, 351
Freudian slip 156
Frijda, Nico 316
Fromm, Erich 170

Gage, Phineas P. 34
Galton, Francis 238
Gardner, Howard 298
gender development 272–4
Gestalt psychology 22, 68, 90, 106, 108, 110–15, 176
Gestalt therapy 176
Gibson, J.J. 138
groups 192–204, 392, 402
groupthink 202, 204
Guthrie, Edwin 70

Hall, G. Stanley 276
happiness 334–5, 378

Harlow, Harry 246
health psychology 386
Hebb, Donald 102
Horney, Karen 170
Hughes, Howard 151
human resource management 398
humanistic psychoanalysis 170
humanistic psychology 354, 358
hypnosis 14, 144, 154, 350

id 146, 147, 150
illusions 138–9
imprinting 86
inferiority complex 164
information processing 118–19, 120, 126, 128–9
ingroups 204, 402
instinct 88
intelligence 288–300, 320
    Cattell-Horn-Carroll theory 296
    cultural and racial prejudices 294–5
    different kinds of 292–3
    fluid and crystallized 296–7
    general vs. specific 290, 292, 298
    multiple intelligences 298–9
    nature vs. nurture 300
Intelligence Quotient (IQ) 288, 289, 290

James, William 36
Janis, Irving 202
Jung, Carl 142, 158, 160–2

Kastenbaum, Robert 284
Kelly, George A. 310
Klein, Melanie 166
Koffa, Kurt 110
Kohlberg, Lawrence 264
Köhler, Wolfgang 106
Kraepelin, Emil 16, 324, 332

Lacan, Jacques 178–9
Laing, R.D. 182
language learning 104
Latané, Bibb 190, 220
Law of Effect 56–7, 58
learned helplessness theory 376, 378
Lewin, Kurt 186, 192–8
libido 150, 152
Little Albert experiment 60, 64, 66, 362
Loftus, Elizabeth 136
Lorenz, Konrad 86, 88, 216

Martin, Dorothy 228
Maslow, Abraham 44, 170, 172, 174, 354–7
May, Rollo 174
meaning of life 172–3
media, learning from the 270
meditation 382
memorizing 94, 130
memory/memories 38, 92–102

different kinds of 130–1
forgetting 96–7, 134
long-term 100–1, 120
recalling 132–3
repressed 136, 152
seven sins of 134–5
short-term 100–1, 120, 122
"storage" of 102–3
unreliable 136
working 120
mental disorders 16–17, 180–1, 182, 320, 322–40, 344, 386
treatment of 342–82
Mesmer, Franz 14
middle age 280
Milgram, Stanley 198, 206, 208–9, 210
Miller, George Armitage 120, 122
Milwaukee project (1968) 300
mind-body dualism 10, 26
mindfulness 382
Mischel, Walter 312
mood disorders 324, 332, 368, 370, 376
moral development 264–5, 266
motivation 44
multiple personality disorder 314

nature vs. nurture debate 62, 238, 240, 300

needs 44, 354, 356–7
nervous system 26–7, 36
neural pathways 28–9
neuroscience 12–13, 24, 38, 342, 404
normality 320

obedience 206, 208, 210, 214
objective approach 48–9
obsessive-compulsive disorder (OCD) 330, 374
occupational psychology 400
old age 282
organizational psychology 392
Other, the 178–9
outgroups 204, 402

paradoxes 138–9
parenting 64–5
pattern recognition 114–15
Pavlov's dog experiments 20–1, 22, 46, 50–1, 52, 58, 70
perception 108–9, 112–13, 176
performance 188, 402
Perls, Fritz and Laura 176
person-centered therapy 358
personal construct theory 310
personality 302–15
Big Five 308–9
extraversion and

neuroticism 306–7
multiple personalities 314–15
and situation 312
trait theory 304, 312
personality disorders 332
persuasion 222, 224, 394
Piaget, Jean 250–6, 264, 396
pleasure principle 172
pop psychology 406
positive psychology 378–9, 380
posttraumatic stress disorder (PTSD) 330, 360
problem solving 106
problems in living 338–9
prosocial behavior 218
psychiatry 180, 182, 342, 344
psychoanalysis 142–85, 350, 352
psychodynamics 142, 342, 354
psychological development, stages of 250–2
psychosexual development, stages of 150, 262
psychosocial development, stages of 262–3
psychotherapy 174, 350, 352, 382
punishment 84
puzzle boxes 52–3, 54, 70, 78

radical behaviorism 72, 86
rational emotive behavior therapy (REBT) 368–9

recall 94, 96, 130, 132, 134
reciprocal inhibition 362
reinforcement
  negative 76, 84, 366
  positive 76, 84
relationships, long-term 234, 278
repression 152, 154
rewards 84
Ringelmann, Max 190
Rogers, Carl 170, 358
Rosenhan, David 340
Rutter, Michael 248

schizophrenia 324, 326
self, concept of 254
Seligman, Martin 376, 378
sensory processes 30–1
separation 240, 242, 244
7, magical number 120–1
Shepard, Roger 138
Sherif, Muzafer 204
Siffre, Michel 40, 41
single lesson 70
situation 214
Skinner, B.F. 72–86, 88, 362
Skinner boxes 78–9
Skinner teaching machine 82–3
sleeping 40, 42–3
social learning theory 266–70, 272
social loafing 190, 219, 402
social psychology 186–234
Spearman, Charles 290
sports psychology 402

Stanford prison experiment 212, 214
Strange Situation experiment 244–5
superego 146, 147, 172
systematic desensitization 364
Szasz, Thomas 180, 182, 338

talking cure 144–5, 156, 176, 342, 350
team leader 196–7
Thorndike, Edward 52, 54, 56
Tolman, Edward 68
transactional analysis 184
True Self 168
Tulving, Endel 130, 132

unconscious 146–7, 148, 152, 154, 158, 172, 178, 350
  collective 160

Vygotsky, Lev 258, 260

wakefulness 40
Watson, John B. 58–66, 88, 224, 246
Wernicke's area 32, 34
Winnicott, Donald 168
Wolpe, Joseph 360, 362, 364
Wundt, Wilhelm 18–19, 22, 90

Zeigarnik effect 98
Zing-Yang Kuo 88

Quercus

New York • London

Text © 2015 by Marcus Weeks
First published in the United States by
Quercus in 2015

ISBN 978-1-62365-483-2

Library of Congress Control Number:
2014948266

Distributed in the United States and Canada
by Hachette Book Group
237 Park Avenue
New York, NY 10017

Manufactured in China

10 9 8 7 6 5 4 3 2 1

www.quercus.com